THE SECRET GOSPEL OF MAXWELL LORD

JUSTICE LEAGUE INTERNATIONAL

Keith Giffen	**PLOTS & BREAKDOWNS**
J.M. DeMatteis	**SCRIPTS**
Kevin Maguire Bill Willingham	**PENCILS**
Al Gordon Dennis Janke P. Craig Russell Bill Wray R. Campanella Bruce Patterson Dick Giordano	**INKS**
Bob Lappan John Workman	**LETTERS**
Gene D'Angelo	**COLORS**

DC COMICS INC.

Jenette Kahn
president & editor-in-chief

Dick Giordano
v.p. - editorial director

Michael Charles Hill
Bob Kahan
editors - collected edition

Andy Helfer
editor - original series

Jim Chadwick
director - design services

Robbin Brosterman
art director

Joe Orlando
v.p. - creative director

Paul Levitz
executive v.p. & publisher

Bruce Bristow
v.p. - sales & marketing

Patrick Caldon
v.p. - controller

Terri Cunningham
director - editorial administration

Chantal d'Aulnis
v.p. - business affairs

Lillian Laserson
v.p. - legal affairs

Bob Rozakis
production director

Cover illustration by Kevin Maguire
Publication design by Dale Crain

THE GOSPEL TRUTH
by helfer

Five years ago, Keith Giffen and I sat down to plot the first issue of the revitalized Justice League. There were a number of things we didn't know at the time. We weren't sure who would dialogue and draw the book. We didn't know precisely which characters would be included in the group. We weren't yet certain how they would come together to form a new and improved Justice League. And most important, we had no idea that the resultant series would become wildly successful and would eventually be reprinted in the volume you now hold in your hands.

But there was one thing we DID know. From the very beginning. Simply put, we knew that however the disparate heroes DID ultimately band together, it would

be due to the machinations of a character we came up with named Maxwell Lord.

Who was Maxwell Lord? To readers of the first issues of Justice League, that was the big question—and truth to tell, at first, his origins were as much a mystery to us as to the readers. We decided to wait a year before revealing Max's secret—and hoped that would be enough time for US to figure out what it was.

In the meantime, we figured we could use Max to do anything we wanted him to do. And what Max did best was manipulate. People. Heroes. The press. World opinion. Anything and everything. He very quickly emerged as the ultimate advance man, marketing wizard, and public relations king all rolled into one. The consummate businessman, no amount of red tape could discourage or dissuade him. He felt as comfortable addressing the United Nations as he did a corporate board of directors. He was a miracle worker. But no one—not the readers, not the world, not even the members of the Justice League itself—knew HOW he did it. Such was the strength of his personality that few characters in the book even thought to question his methods. So sincere, so convincing...so...salesmanlike was Maxwell Lord, he inspired instant trust in all but the most skeptical super-hero.

In the first few issues of JUSTICE LEAGUE, readers gradually discovered that Maxwell Lord was the driving force behind the League. In the first issue alone, he not only manages to bring the League together to fight a terrorist threat, but also indirectly masterminded the threat in the first place. From his desk inside the offices of "Innovative Concepts, Inc." he monitored the action in the United Nations as it unfolded, all the while absently doodling variations on the name he'd soon give to his personal super-hero team.

In issue two, while the Justice League were still trying to figure out who invited each of them to join the new League, Max initiated plans to recruit additional members to the group. Still, it wasn't until the end of the third issue that the League finally met Maxwell Lord—as Lord presented them with his latest member for the team: Booster Gold. Although at first reluctant to accept him, Booster's handling of the Royal Flush gang (who, for unknown reasons, happened to be lurking just outside the League's headquarters, waiting for the moment to attack) convinced the group that their initial judgment might have been a bit hasty.

Their lineup stable for the moment, the League, led by Batman, then tried to find out a bit of background on Max. But the files were pretty much bare. Still, suspicions were on the rise, and as Max's plan proceeded (with a few hitches.) Keith, aided and abetted by scripter J. M. DeMatteis, began to edge his way to the point of the Max Lord storyline.

The first real clues surfaced in issue seven. After a particularly messy incursion into Russia back in issues two and three, world approval of the Justice League was at an all-time low. An isolated computer terminal, after running some probability checks, ultimately determined that, given current factors, U.N. acceptance of a mysterious "proposal" was unlikely. The computer decided to "change the odds" and, in response, a subspace satellite suddenly began spewing a deadly heat beam across the face of the planet—its destination a string of nuclear installations on the European continent. Oddly enough, Max Lord seemed as disturbed by this turn of events as anyone else. Disturbed...but not quite surprised.

Of course, the Justice League flew up into space to head off the disaster by destroying the satellite—but before they did, Mister Miracle made a pair of puzzling discoveries: first, that the satellite was equipped with video cameras that had been recording the group's every heroic gesture; and second, that the satellite itself could only have been created by someone or something with extensive knowledge of Apokoliptian weapons design. (For those readers out there who have no idea what "Apokoliptian design" is, suffice it to say it's the meanest other-worldly place in the DC Universe, and happens to be Mister Miracle's home planet.)

By the end of the issue, however, both points had been forgotten: the Security Council of the U.N.—and indeed, the entire world—had witnessed the heroism of the Justice League, and had decided to issue U.N. sanctioning to the group. The "proposal" was passed—and Maxwell Lord finally got what he wanted all along: Justice League International.

Which brings us up to the issues reprinted in the current volume. After the rather tasty double-sized annual story which directly follows this introduction, you'll dive back into the Maxwell Lord storyline, which culminates with the two-part story in issues eleven and twelve. Before those two stories, however, there's a one-off, change of pace issue ("Moving Day," which proved to be our most popular single issue, and served as the standard for the Justice League's peculiar brand of humor for years to come) and a pair of digressive (but battle-fraught) crossover stories (with supplementary material provided by Kevin Dooley—just so you can understand what's going on without benefit of scorecard). Then it's wrap-up time, where you will finally discover (or rediscover, if this is your second time around) the truth about Maxwell Lord—a truth even the writers, artists and editors of Justice League weren't quite sure of until it was over.

Now, let's be honest here: Was it really possible that no one involved in the creative process of this book actually knew how it was all going to turn out? Was it possible that Keith Giffen could have vamped a crucial storyline for ten issues, dropping clues along the way without knowing what they were clues to? And finally, was it possible that a writer could have taken all those disparate clues and sewed them up seamlessly into a revelatory sequence that made the whole affair seem as though it was planned from the very beginning? Well, you can choose to believe it or not, but that's the way it happened. Keith and J.M. pulled it off. Flawlessly, to these editorial eyes. Kevin and Al drew it (equally flawlessly, I might add) and when the issues finally came out, everyone thought we were the hardest working, most conscientious crew in the comics business. All that planning, all that stringing along, all those tantalizing clues that actually proved to be significant...

Yeah, right. Maxwell Lord might be the consummate comic book showman—but he met his real-life equivalent in Keith Giffen.

And that, dear readers, is the gospel truth.

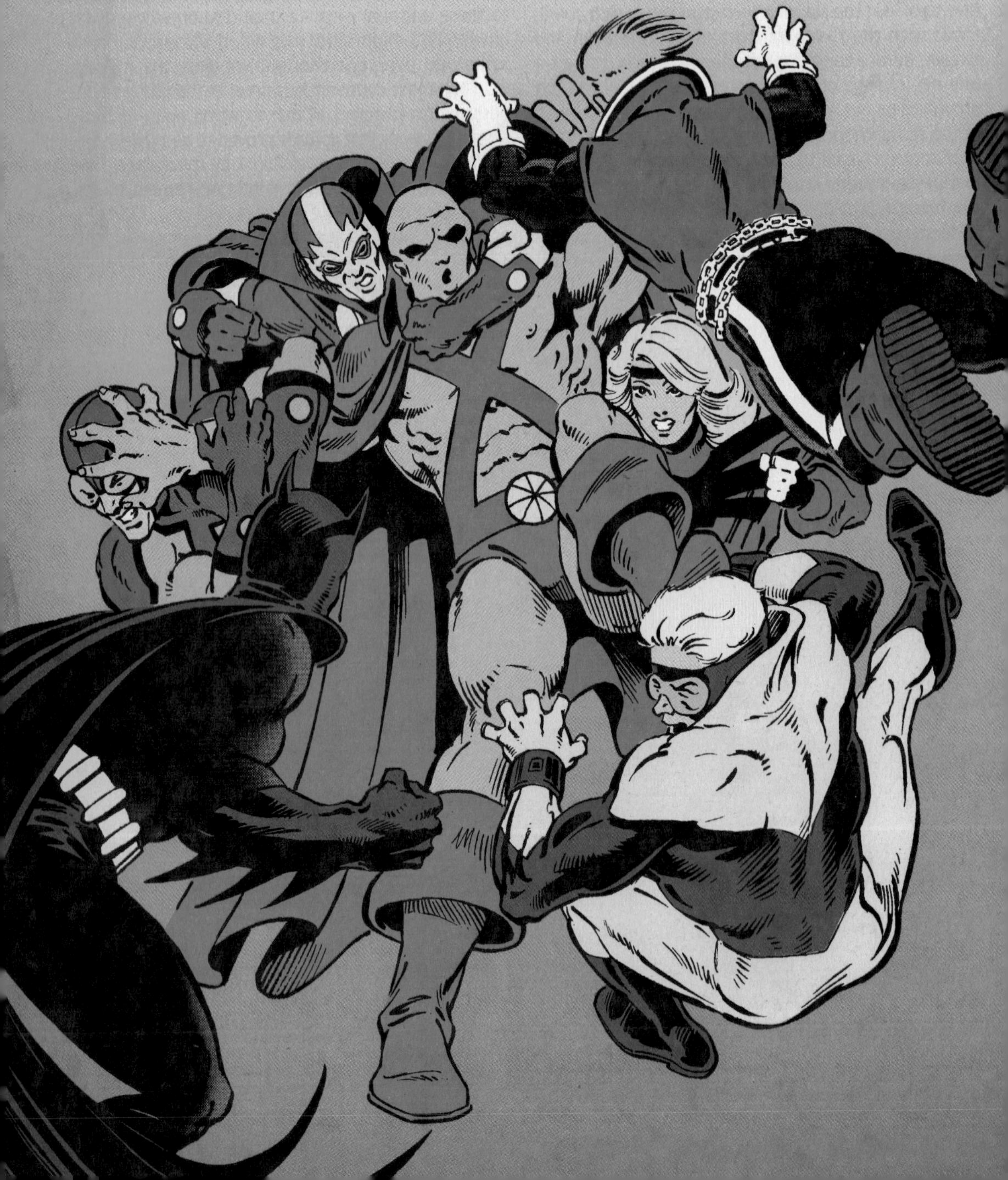

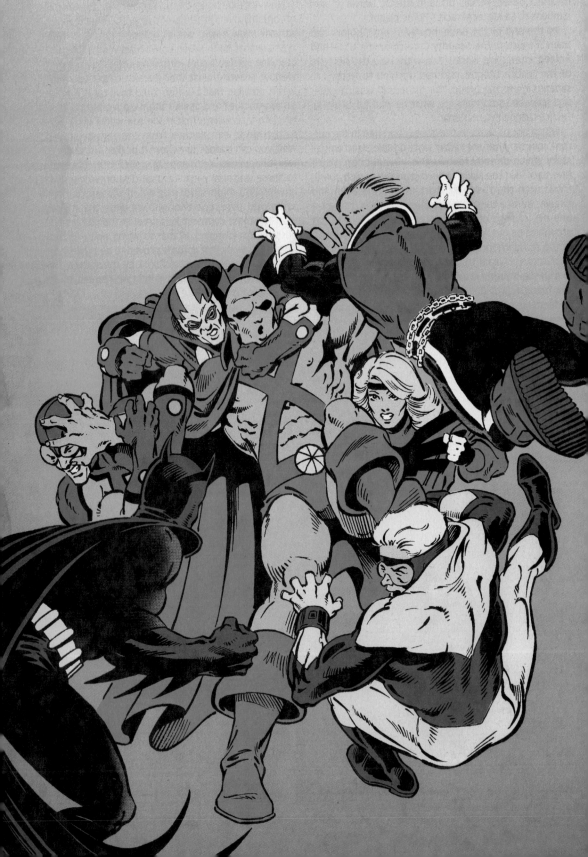

SOMEWHERE IN THE SOUTH PACIFIC...

COULD SOMEBODY *PLEASE* TELL ME WHAT WE'RE DOIN' HERE?

I MEAN, FOR CRYIN' OUT LOUD, THIS MAKES *NOWHERE* LOOK LIKE *SOMEWHERE.*

COOL YOUR JETS, HERBERT.

IT'S TOO *HOT* TO COOL MY JETS.

THEN HOW ABOUT JUST SHUTTING *UP?*

THIS WAY, FELLAS. MAIN COMPOUND'S DEAD AHEAD.

I NEED A BEER.

nTECH™
BUILDING LIFE FROM LIFE

PRIVATE PROPERTY

I DON'T THINK YOU'LL FIND ANY AROUND HERE.

FAR AS I KNOW, KORD JUST BOUGHT THIS COMPLEX A COUPLE O' WEEKS AGO--AN' IT'S BEEN *DESERTED* FOR A COUPLE O' *YEARS.*

SO WHAT'D HE *BUY* IT FOR?

HOW THE HECK SHOULD *I* KNOW?

WE'RE BEIN' PAID TO CHECK IT OUT--

SO LET'S START *CHECKIN'.*

JEEZ-- WILL YOU *LOOK* AT THIS PLACE?

WHAT *WAS* THIS JOINT BEFORE, ANYWAY?

SOME KIND OF *RESEARCH FACILITY,* THAT'S ALL *I* KNOW. PART OF A LARGER COMPANY THAT KORO ABSORBED.

WASN'T THERE A "STAR TREK" LIKE THIS? KIRK, SPOCK AN' MCCOY BEAM DOWN TO SOME ABANDONED RESEARCH FACILITY AN' THE NEXT THING YOU KNOW--

DOO DOO DOO DOO DOO DOO DOO DOO--

THAT'S THE *"TWILIGHT ZONE"* THEME, JERK.

OH, YEAH. YOU'RE RIGHT.

C'MON LET'S JUST DO THE JOB AND GET THE HECK *OUT* OF HERE.

GEEZ... WHAT A MESS.

IT'S TOO QUIET AROUND HERE. DOESN'T ANYBODY *LIVE* ON THIS ISLAND?

GIVEN A CHOICE-- WOULD *YOU* STICK AROUND A DUMP LIKE THIS?

HEY... UH... PHILLIPS?

WHAT?

WE GOT *COMPANY.*

SHE GAZES INTO THEIR EYES...

...AND THEY UNDERSTAND.

SO THEY FLY OFF... MY MESSENGERS... MY *ANGELS.*

FLY OFF TO SPREAD MY *GOSPEL.*

TO CONVERT THE MASSES TO MY *CAUSE.*

FLY.

WHUP WHUP WHUP WHUP WHUP WHUP WHUP WH

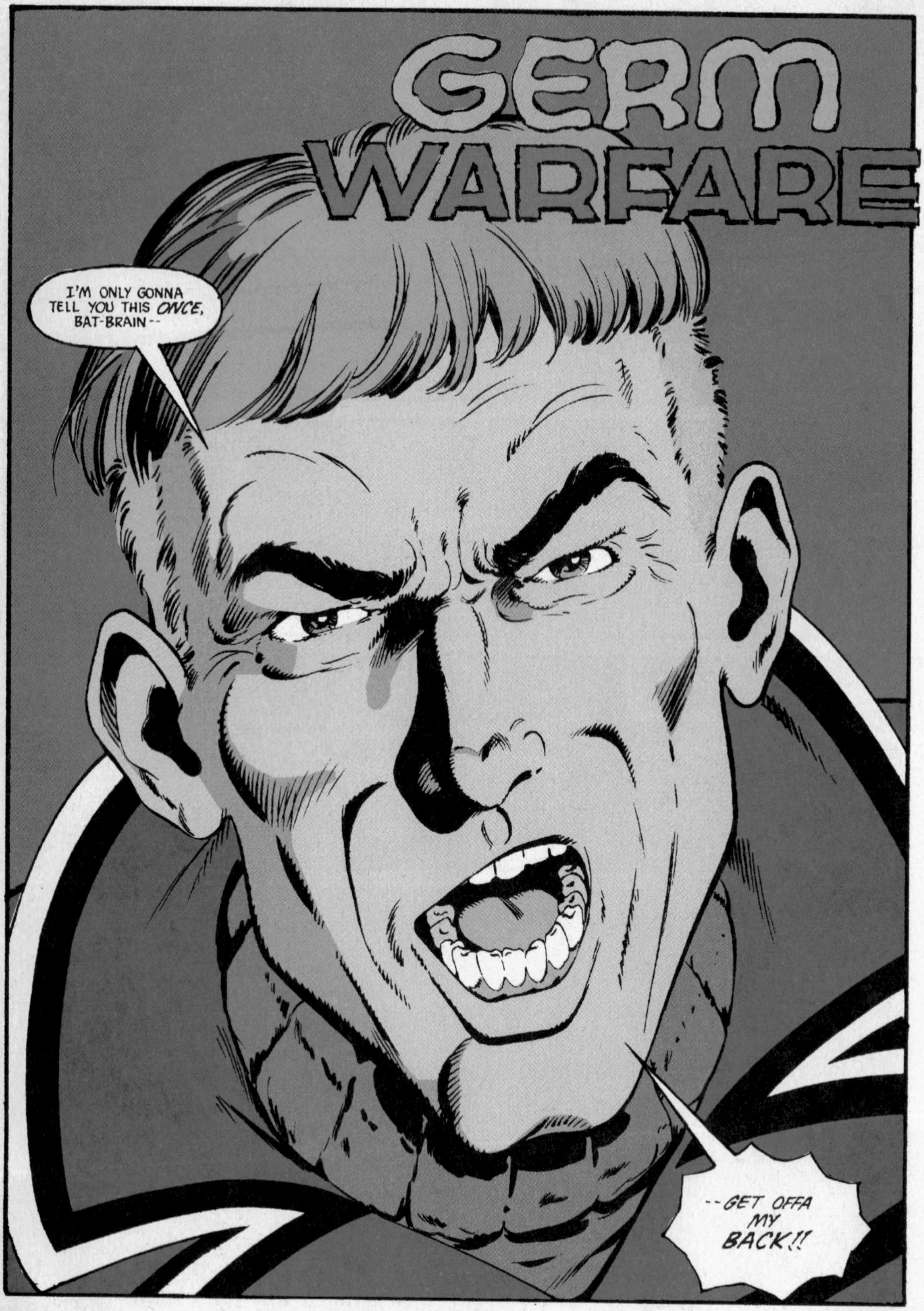
GERM WARFARE
I'M ONLY GONNA TELL YOU THIS ONCE, BAT-BRAIN--
--GET OFFA MY BACK!!

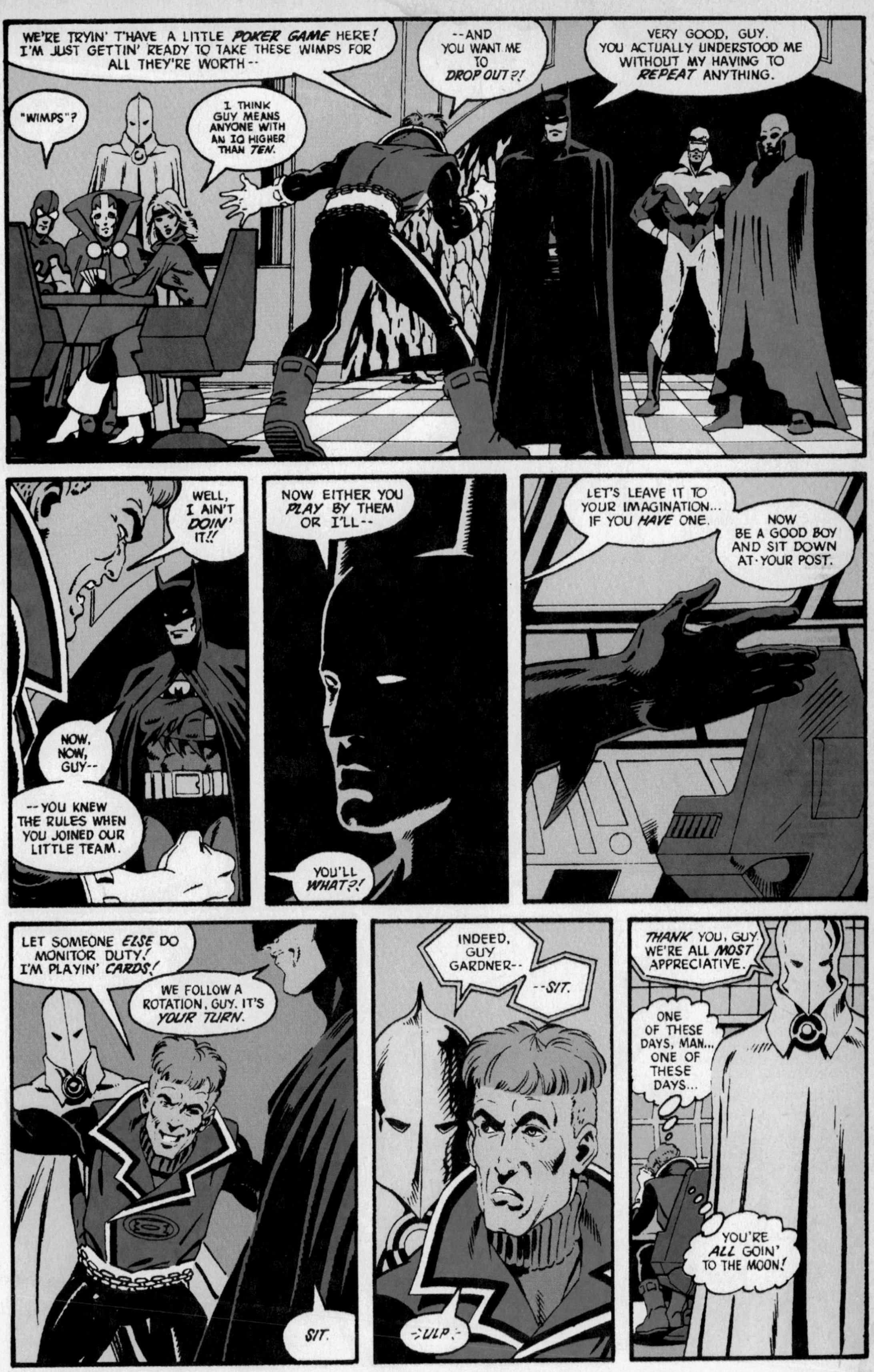
WE'RE TRYIN' T'HAVE A LITTLE POKER GAME HERE! I'M JUST GETTIN' READY TO TAKE THESE WIMPS FOR ALL THEY'RE WORTH--
"WIMPS"?
I THINK GUY MEANS ANYONE WITH AN IQ HIGHER THAN TEN.
--AND YOU WANT ME TO DROP OUT?!
VERY GOOD, GUY. YOU ACTUALLY UNDERSTOOD ME WITHOUT MY HAVING TO REPEAT ANYTHING.
WELL, I AIN'T DOIN' IT!!
NOW, NOW, GUY--
--YOU KNEW THE RULES WHEN YOU JOINED OUR LITTLE TEAM.
NOW EITHER YOU PLAY BY THEM OR I'LL--
YOU'LL WHAT?!
LET'S LEAVE IT TO YOUR IMAGINATION... IF YOU HAVE ONE.
NOW BE A GOOD BOY AND SIT DOWN AT YOUR POST.
LET SOMEONE ELSE DO MONITOR DUTY! I'M PLAYIN' CARDS!
WE FOLLOW A ROTATION, GUY. IT'S YOUR TURN.
SIT.
INDEED, GUY GARDNER--
--SIT.
ULP
THANK YOU, GUY. WE'RE ALL MOST APPRECIATIVE.
ONE OF THESE DAYS, MAN... ONE OF THESE DAYS...
YOU'RE ALL GOIN' TO THE MOON!

BATMAN'S SO FULL OF HIMSELF HE'S GONNA EXPLODE... AND THAT DOCTOR FATE... (((BRRRR)))...

...HE AIN'T EVEN *HUMAN*. LEAST I DON'T THINK HE IS. I FEEL A *COLD DRAFT* EVERY TIME HE STANDS *NEXT* TO ME.

NOW, IF WE COULD GET DOWN TO BUSINESS...

BUT GIVE ME A LITTLE TIME AND I'LL PUT 'EM *ALL* IN LINE. I'LL BE RUNNIN' THIS LEAGUE AN' I'LL BE RUNNIN' IT --

EMERGENCY ALERT:
COMPUTER-CORRELATED DANGER FACTOR EIGHT
PARIS...
LOS ANGELES...
SYDNEY...
TOKYO...
LARGE POPULATION SEGMENTS SEEMINGLY UNDER CONTROL OF OUTSIDE FORCE...

...RIGHT...?!

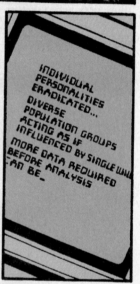

INDIVIDUAL PERSONALITIES ERADICATED... DIVERSE POPULATION GROUPS ACTING AS IF INFLUENCED BY SINGLE WILL... MORE DATA REQUIRED BEFORE ANALYSIS CAN BE —

YO... BIG-EARS!

GARDNER-- *FORGET* THE CARD GAME!

THIS HASN'T GOT ANYTHING TO *DO* WITH THE CARD GAME! YOU WANTED ME MONITORING, RIGHT?

WELL, I JUST MONITORED MYSELF A *DOOZY*!

IDENTICAL OCCURRENCES IN FOUR DIFFERENT LOCATIONS. NO APPARENT LINKS, AND YET...

12

MANHUNTER... COME HAVE A LOOK AT THIS.

INDIVIDUAL PERSONALITIES ERADICATED...

DIVERSE POPULATION GROUPS ACTING AS IF INFLUENCED BY SINGLE WILL

MORE DATA REQUIRED BEFORE ANALYSIS

WHAT DO YOU *THINK,* J'ONN? IS THIS LEAGUE BUSINESS?

..NOBODY ASKED.

WELL, I'LL TELL YA WHAT *I* THINK--

THE COMPUTER WAS PROGRAMMED TO BRING POSSIBLE CRISIS SITUATIONS TO OUR ATTENTION. AT THE VERY *LEAST,* WE SHOULD *INVESTIGATE...*

BUT ZOMBIE-LIKE BEHAVIOR ALONE ISN'T NECESSARILY GROUNDS FOR *OUR* INVOLVEMENT --

YEAH. FOR ALL WE KNOW THIS COULD BE SOME KIND OF TEMPORARY PHENOMENON... SOME WEIRD COINCIDENCE THAT--

GOOD POINT, *BEETLE.*

MISTER MIRACLE -- YOU PROGRAMMED THE COMPUTER. COULD THIS JUST BE SOME ODD COINCIDENCE OR --

ABSOLUTELY NOT. THE COMPUTER WILL *COMPENSATE* FOR RANDOM OCCURRENCES. IF THIS WASN'T A GENUINE THREAT --

IT WOULDN'T HAVE COME UP. YES, I *KNOW* THAT.

SO WHY ARE YOU WASTING OUR TIME *TALKING* ABOUT IT?

I WANTED YOU ALL TO FEEL *INCLUDED* IN THE DECISION-MAKING PROCESS.

WELL, IF THAT'S THE CASE, HERE'S WHAT *I* THINK WE SHOULD DO.

I SAID I WANTED YOU TO FEEL *INCLUDED* IN THE DECISION-MAKING PROCESS. I DIDN'T SAY YOU SHOULD *USURP* IT.

BUT--!

NOW HERE'S WHAT WE'LL *DO...*

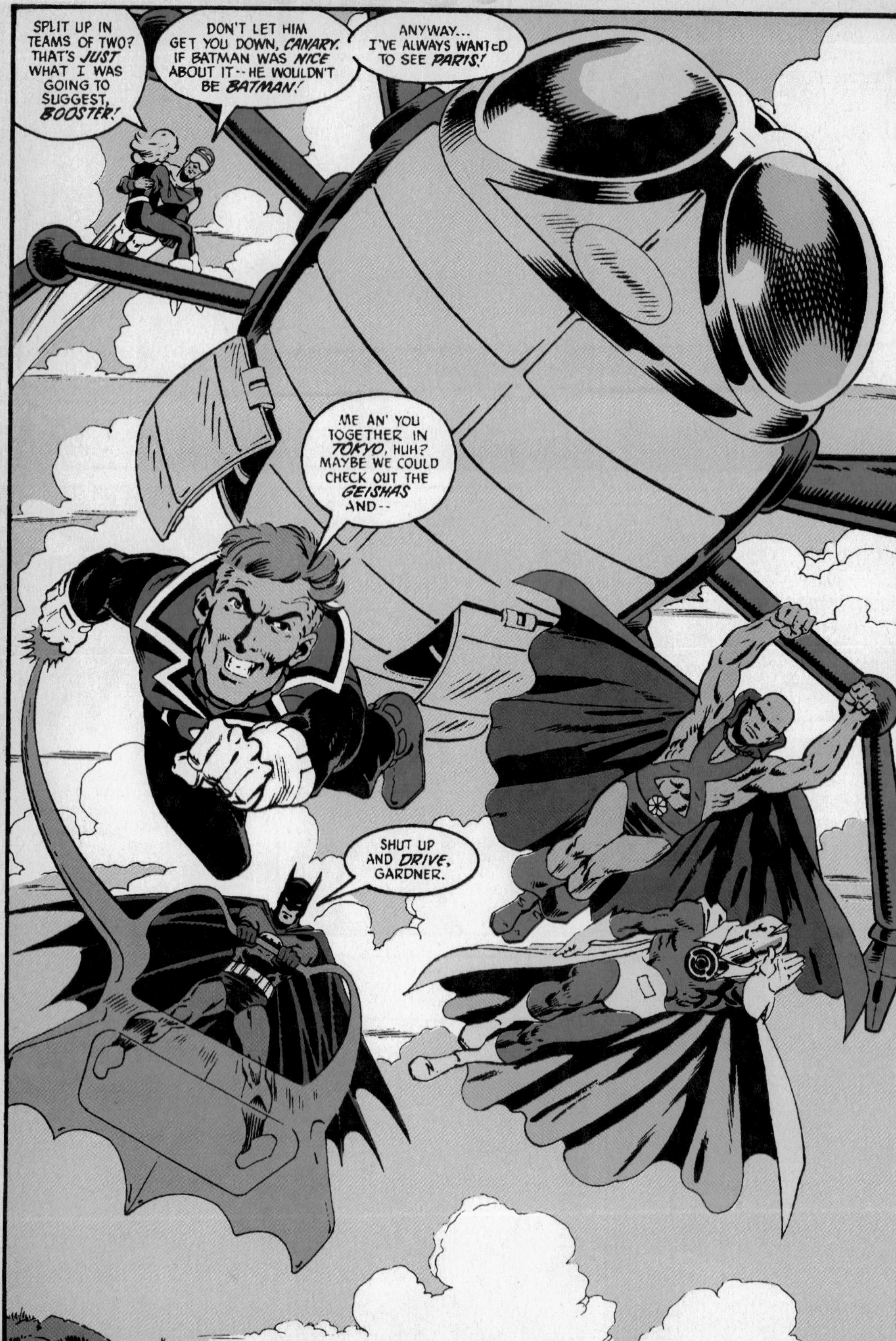
SPLIT UP IN TEAMS OF TWO? THAT'S JUST WHAT I WAS GOING TO SUGGEST, BOOSTER!
DON'T LET HIM GET YOU DOWN, CANARY. IF BATMAN WAS NICE ABOUT IT--HE WOULDN'T BE BATMAN!
ANYWAY... I'VE ALWAYS WANTED TO SEE PARIS!
ME AN' YOU TOGETHER IN TOKYO, HUH? MAYBE WE COULD CHECK OUT THE GEISHAS AND--
SHUT UP AND DRIVE, GARDNER.

...HOLLYWOOOOD HERE WE COME!

THE LOS ANGELES AND TOKYO PROBLEMS ARE CENTERED AT "KORD INDUSTRIES" PLANTS, AREN'T THEY, BEETLE?

MMMMM. THAT'S WHY BATMAN'S SENDING ME OUT TO LA-LA LAND. AS TED KORD, I AM "KORD INDUSTRIES."

SO HOW DO YOU FIND THE TIME FOR SUPER-HEROING?

HEY-- THIS IS THE 'BOS! A GUY CAN BE AN EXECUTIVE AND A SUPER-HERO AND HAVE A FULFILLING PERSONAL LIFE AND --

HOW DO YOU DO IT?

NERVOUS BREAKDOWN EVERY SECOND SUNDAY.

...Y'KNOW, THIS WOULD HAVE BEEN FASTER IF YOU'D LET DR. FATE ZAP US THERE.

THAT'S HOW THE OTHERS ARE COVERING SUCH GREAT DISTANCES.

ZAP, SHMAP!

JUST WATCH THIS BABY MOVE!!

WHOOO

NICE PICK-UP, HUH?

YOU THINK MAYBE YOU COULD PICK ME UP?

STAY THAT WAY. THEY'LL LOVE YOU IN L.A.!

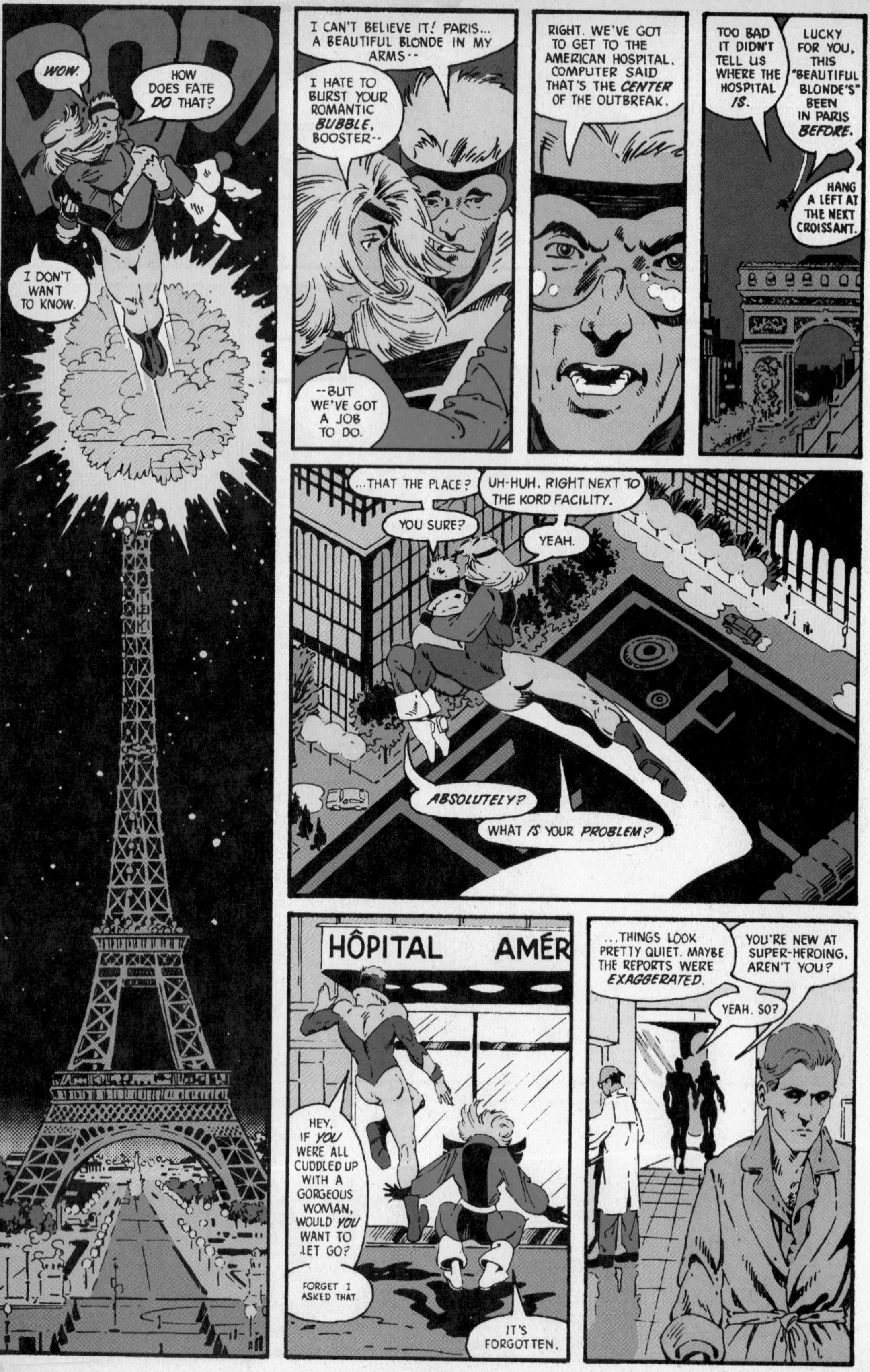
POP!
WOW.
HOW DOES FATE DO THAT?
I DON'T WANT TO KNOW.
I CAN'T BELIEVE IT! PARIS... A BEAUTIFUL BLONDE IN MY ARMS--
I HATE TO BURST YOUR ROMANTIC BUBBLE, BOOSTER--
--BUT WE'VE GOT A JOB TO DO.
RIGHT. WE'VE GOT TO GET TO THE AMERICAN HOSPITAL. COMPUTER SAID THAT'S THE CENTER OF THE OUTBREAK.
TOO BAD IT DIDN'T TELL US WHERE THE HOSPITAL IS.
LUCKY FOR YOU, THIS "BEAUTIFUL BLONDE'S" BEEN IN PARIS BEFORE.
HANG A LEFT AT THE NEXT CROISSANT.
...THAT THE PLACE?
UH-HUH. RIGHT NEXT TO THE KORD FACILITY.
YOU SURE?
YEAH.
ABSOLUTELY?
WHAT IS YOUR PROBLEM?
HÔPITAL AMÉR
HEY, IF YOU WERE ALL CUDDLED UP WITH A GORGEOUS WOMAN, WOULD YOU WANT TO LET GO?
FORGET I ASKED THAT.
IT'S FORGOTTEN.
...THINGS LOOK PRETTY QUIET. MAYBE THE REPORTS WERE EXAGGERATED.
YOU'RE NEW AT SUPER-HEROING, AREN'T YOU?
YEAH. SO?

ONE OF THE FIRST THINGS YOU LEARN IN THIS GAME IS THAT THE *QUIETER* THINGS ARE-- THE *WORSE* THEY'RE PROBABLY GOING TO GET.

BEAUTIFUL-- AND WISE, TOO. WOWSER-- WHAT A *COMBINATION!*

I'M ALSO REALLY GOOD AT BREAKING *LIMBS.*

I'LL KEEP THAT IN *MIND.*

NOW COME ON-- LET'S GO FIND THE HOSPITAL *DIRECTOR.*

THAT IS, IF THESE PEOPLE WILL *LET* US.

LOOK AT THEIR *EYES,* CANARY... IT'S LIKE THEY'RE *DEAD* INSIDE!

WHATEVER'S INFECTED THEM-- I GET THE FEELING THEY WANT TO PASS IT *ON!*

I *TOLD* YOU, IT'S *WORSE* WHEN THINGS ARE QUIET.

ATTENDEZ S'IL VOUS PLAIT

AND I'LL NEVER *FORGET* IT--

--PROVIDING WE LIVE *THROUGH* THIS!

REMEMBER: DEFEND YOURSELF, BUT DON'T *HURT* THEM! THEY'RE NOT RESPONSIBLE FOR THEIR--

17

ACTIONS...

THEN AGAIN-- MAYBE THAT'S NOT SUCH A GOOD IDEA.

DON'T SWEAT IT I'VE *GOT* YOU!

BUT *NOW* WHAT?

WE'VE GOT TO GET... CLEAR OF THEM.

CANARY-- ARE YOU ALL RIGHT? YOU SOUND--

I'M... FINE. JUST A LITTLE *DIZZY*--

GUESS THIS MOVE ISN'T HELPING ANY, RIGHT?

NO-- IT'S JUST... WHEN *THEY* SWEPT *OVER* ME, I --

UH-- LOOKS LIKE THEY'RE GONNA BE SWEEPING OVER *BOTH* OF US IN A SECOND--

--UNLESS...

RAKKKKK

MY LUCK, I'LL PROBABLY GET *SUED* FOR PROPERTY DAMAGE.

HURRY!

18

YOU...UH...*MIGHT* WANT TO OPEN THAT *DOOR* THERE. I DON'T KNOW HOW LONG I CAN HOLD THEM!

OH, LORD...

CANARY-- THE *DOOR!*

RIGHT *GOT* IT!

NOW I'VE GOT TO TIME THIS JUST RIGHT:

A-ONE... A-*TWO*... A--

SLAM

--*THREE!!*

SLAM IT! NOW!

AND FOR HEAVEN'S SAKE, MAKE SURE IT'S *LOCKED!*

THAT'S FUNNY. I DON'T HEAR THEM TRYING TO BATTER THE DOOR *DOWN* OR ANYTHING...

HEY-- LOOKS LIKE WE'VE STUMBLED INTO SOMEONE'S ROOM. *SORRY* ABOUT THAT...

IT'S QUITE ALL RIGHT. STAY AS LONG AS YOU'D *LIKE.*

MAYBE WE'LL STAY *FOREVER.*

CANARY-- YOUR *VOICE*--! WHAT ARE YOU...?

OH, I *UNDERSTAND* NOW.

OF *COURSE* YOU DO.

POP

NOW REMEMBER TO *BEHAVE*, GUY...

STOP TALKIN' T'ME LIKE I'M *EIGHT* YEARS OLD! I'M A *GREEN LANTERN*--

TREAT ME WITH *RESPECT!*

I ABSOLUTELY *WILL*--

--AS SOON AS YOU *EARN* IT.

AW, FER--!

WHERE'RE WE *GOIN'*? SUSHI JOINT?

A RESEARCH CENTER IN DOWNTOWN TOKYO. ACCORDING TO THE COMPUTER, IT'S THE *SOURCE* OF THIS "CONTAGION."

DOCTOR LIGHT WORKS HERE-- SHE MIGHT BE ABLE TO HELP US.

AFTER THE WAY *YOU* TREATED HER *--WE'LL BE LUCKY IF SHE DOESN'T RUN US THROUGH WITH A SAMURAI SWORD!

HEY-- THERE SHE *IS!* AND SHE BROUGHT THE WELCOME WAGON!

BATMAN... GUY...

...IT'S *SOOOO* NICE TO SEE YOU AGAIN.

GARDNER-- GET US *OUT* OF HERE... FAST!

IT'S A--

20

--TRAP.

I CAN'T *SEE,* BATS!

I CAN'T *SEE!*

GENTLY NOW, CHILDREN. *GENTLY.*

INTRODUCE YOURSELVES.

MAKE OUR GUESTS FEEL *WELCOME.*

THEY'LL BE *RESISTANT* AT FIRST-- JUST AS *YOU* WERE.

BUT THEY'LL *LEARN.*

THEY'LL *LEARN.*

...STILL CAN'T *SEE* TOO STRAIGHT-- BUT THIS BEASTIE'S OUT TO FLATTEN EVERY LAST *ONE* OF--

GUY-- *NO!*

WHAT DO YOU *MEAN,* "GUY-- NO"?

I'M SAVIN' YOUR *TAIL,* FEARLESS LEADER!

THOSE ARE *INNOCENT PEOPLE!*

NOT THE WAY *I* SEE IT!

I'M IN *CHARGE* HERE, GARDNER! YOU CAN USE YOUR RING TO *CONTAIN* THEM-- BUT DO NOT... I REPEAT... *DO NOT* HURT THEM!

Y'KNOW, I DON'T THINK I'M *EVER* GONNA FIGURE YOU OUT!

THANK HEAVEN FOR *THAT.*

OH, *TERRIFIC!*

YOU'RE BUSY LECTURIN' ME ON *MORALITY*--AND OUR *PAL* WHIPS UP A *YELLOW LIGHT* TO NEUTRALIZE MY *POWER RING!*

OKAY, LADY-- NOW I'M *MAD!* AND WHEN GUY GARDNER'S MAD, AIN'T *NOBODY* CAN STAND IN HIS--

SOK!

OUCH

I WON'T GO DOWN AS *EASILY*, DOCTOR.

I HAVE NO DESIRE TO *HARM* YOU, BATMAN. WHY *SHOULD* I? I...

I *LOVE* YOU!

NO WHAT ARE YOU--?

...MMMMM...

AND I... I LOVE YOU, TOO.

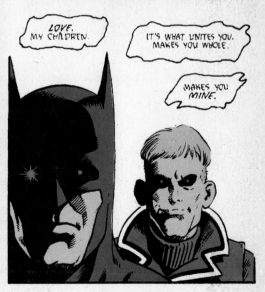

LOVE, MY CHILDREN.

IT'S WHAT UNITES YOU. MAKES YOU WHOLE.

MAKES YOU *MINE.*

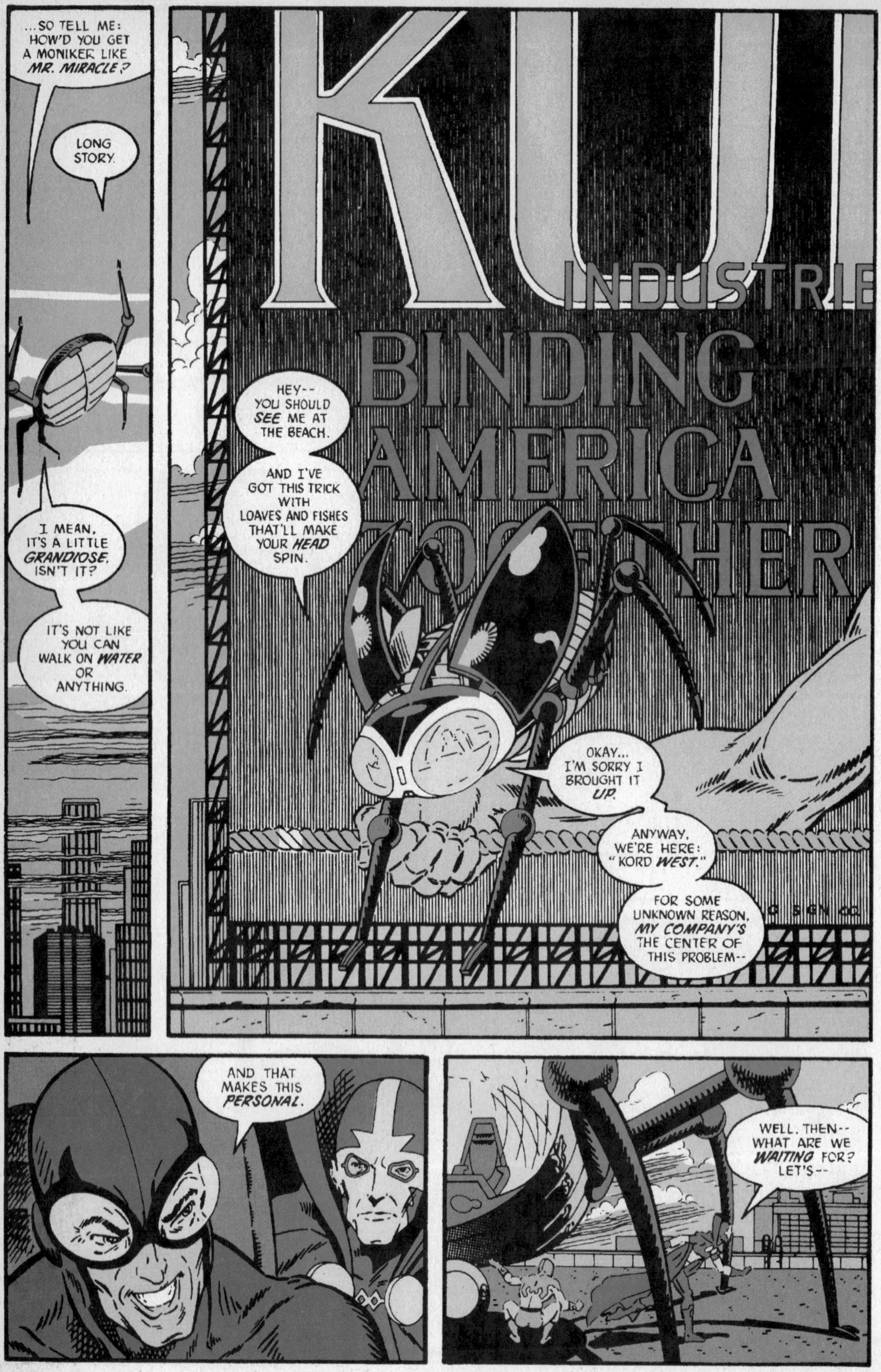
...SO TELL ME: HOW'D YOU GET A MONIKER LIKE *MR. MIRACLE?*
LONG STORY.
I MEAN, IT'S A LITTLE *GRANDIOSE*, ISN'T IT?
IT'S NOT LIKE YOU CAN WALK ON *WATER* OR ANYTHING.
INDUSTRIE
BINDING
AMERICA
HEY-- YOU SHOULD *SEE* ME AT THE BEACH.
AND I'VE GOT THIS TRICK WITH LOAVES AND FISHES THAT'LL MAKE YOUR *HEAD* SPIN.
OKAY... I'M SORRY I BROUGHT IT *UP*.
ANYWAY, WE'RE HERE: "KORD *WEST*."
FOR SOME UNKNOWN REASON, *MY COMPANY'S* THE CENTER OF THIS PROBLEM--
AND THAT MAKES THIS *PERSONAL*.
WELL, THEN-- WHAT ARE WE *WAITING* FOR? LET'S--

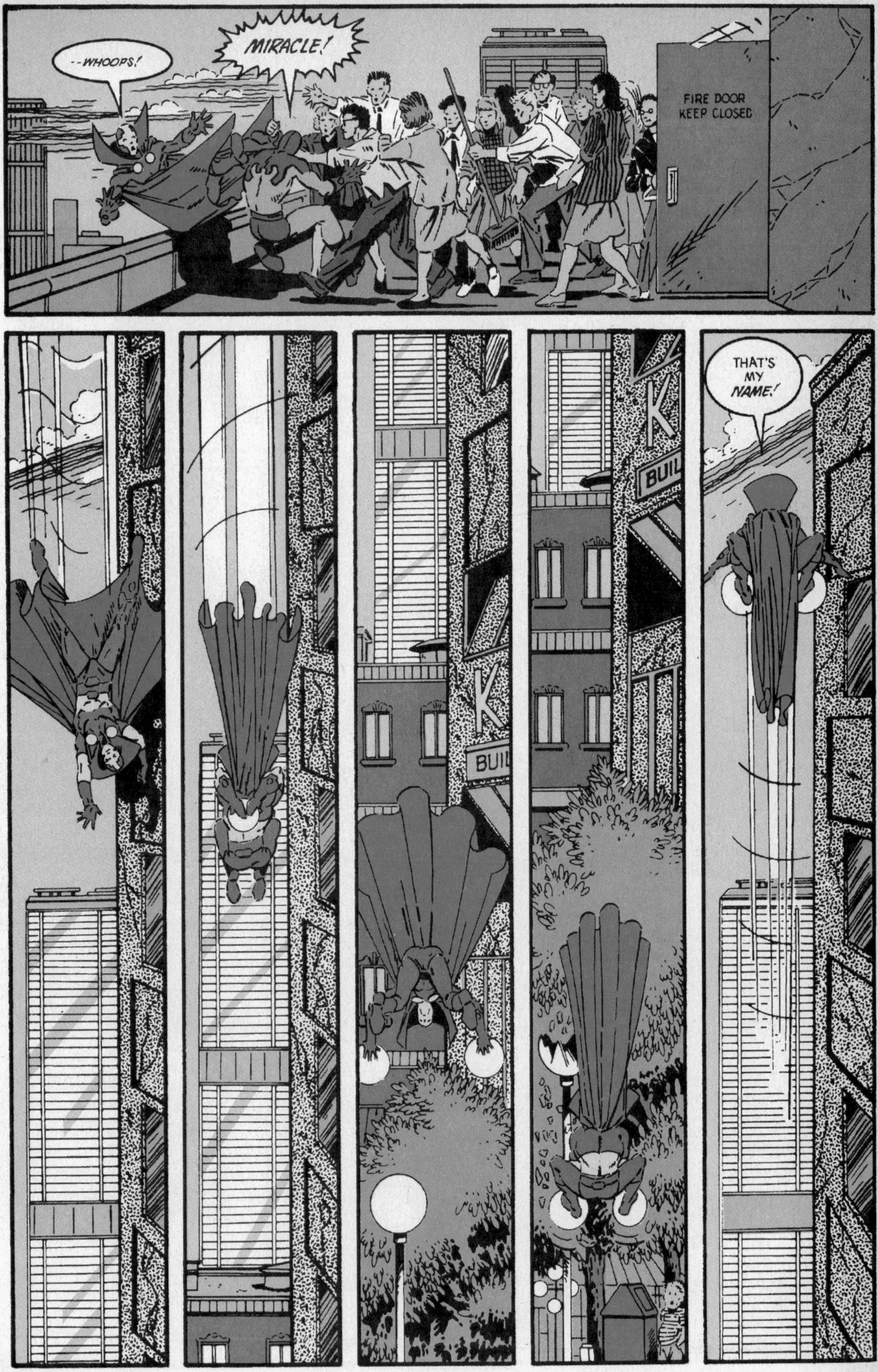
--WHOOPS!
MIRACLE!
FIRE DOOR
KEEP CLOSED
THAT'S MY NAME!

THOSE PEOPLE... LIKE THE *DRONES* IN DARKSEID'S *FIRE-PITS!* NO MINDS OF THEIR OWN-- NO WILL AT *ALL!*

ALTHOUGH FROM WHAT I HEAR ABOUT SOUTHERN CALIFORNIA-- THAT'S NOT ALL THAT *UNUSUAL!*

BEETLE-- DO YOU NEED *HELP?*

TAKE A WILD *GUESS!*

NUTS!

I CAN'T *FIGHT* THESE PEOPLE-- I *KNOW* MOST OF THEM... THEY'RE *FRIENDS!*

WHICH MEANS THE WISEST COURSE IS TO BEAT A HASTY *RETREAT*-- TILL WE CAN FIGURE OUT WHAT'S GOING *ON* HERE AND *WHY!*

HERE, LITTLE "BUG"! COME *ON*, BOY!

THAT'S A *GOOD* "BUG"!

AND I DON'T EVEN HAVE TO *WALK* IT TWICE A DAY!

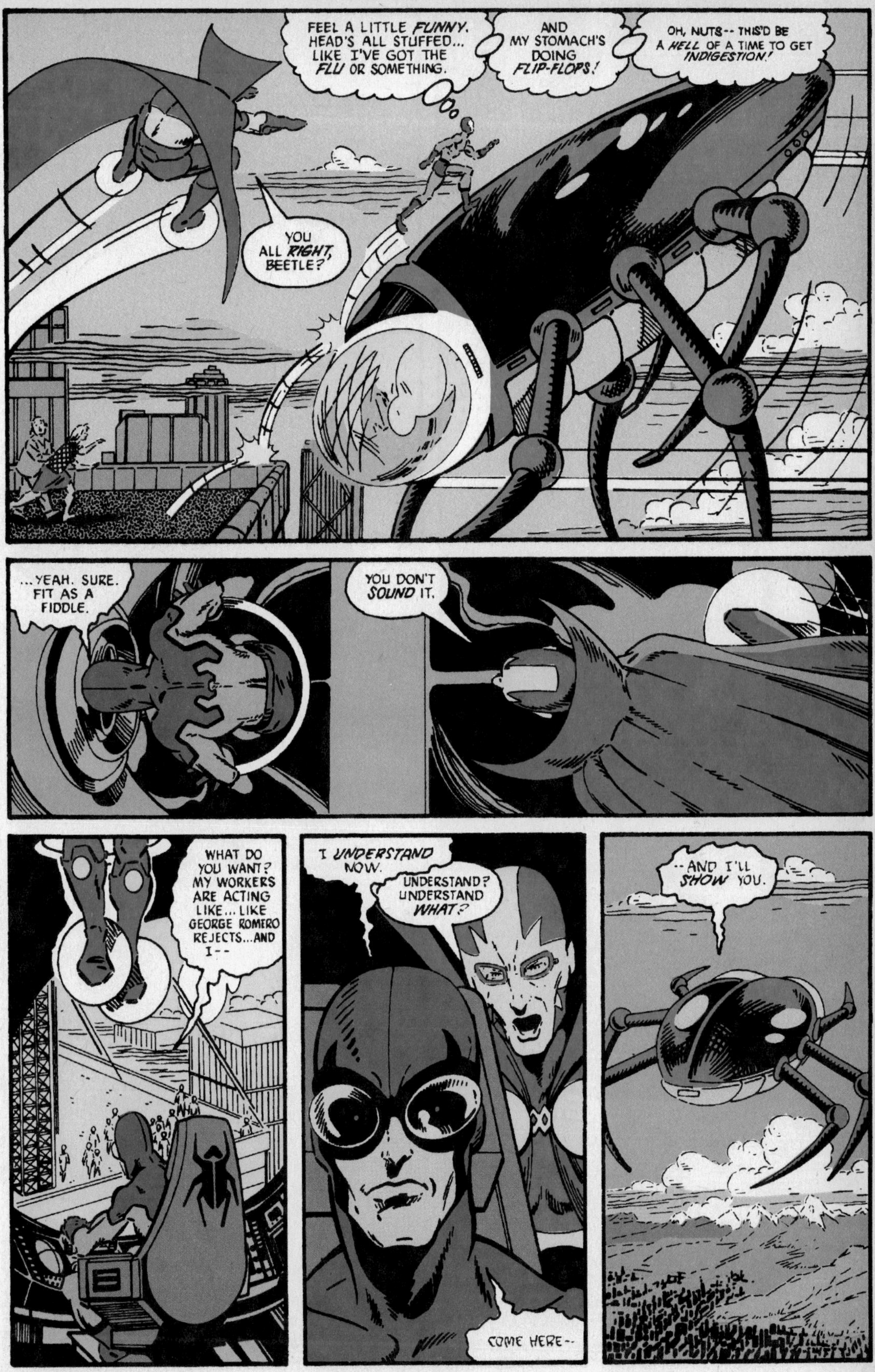
FEEL A LITTLE FUNNY. HEAD'S ALL STUFFED... LIKE I'VE GOT THE FLU OR SOMETHING.
AND MY STOMACH'S DOING FLIP-FLOPS!
OH, NUTS-- THIS'D BE A HELL OF A TIME TO GET INDIGESTION!
YOU ALL RIGHT, BEETLE?
...YEAH. SURE. FIT AS A FIDDLE.
YOU DON'T SOUND IT.
WHAT DO YOU WANT? MY WORKERS ARE ACTING LIKE... LIKE GEORGE ROMERO REJECTS...AND I--
I UNDERSTAND NOW.
UNDERSTAND? UNDERSTAND WHAT?
COME HERE--
--AND I'LL SHOW YOU.

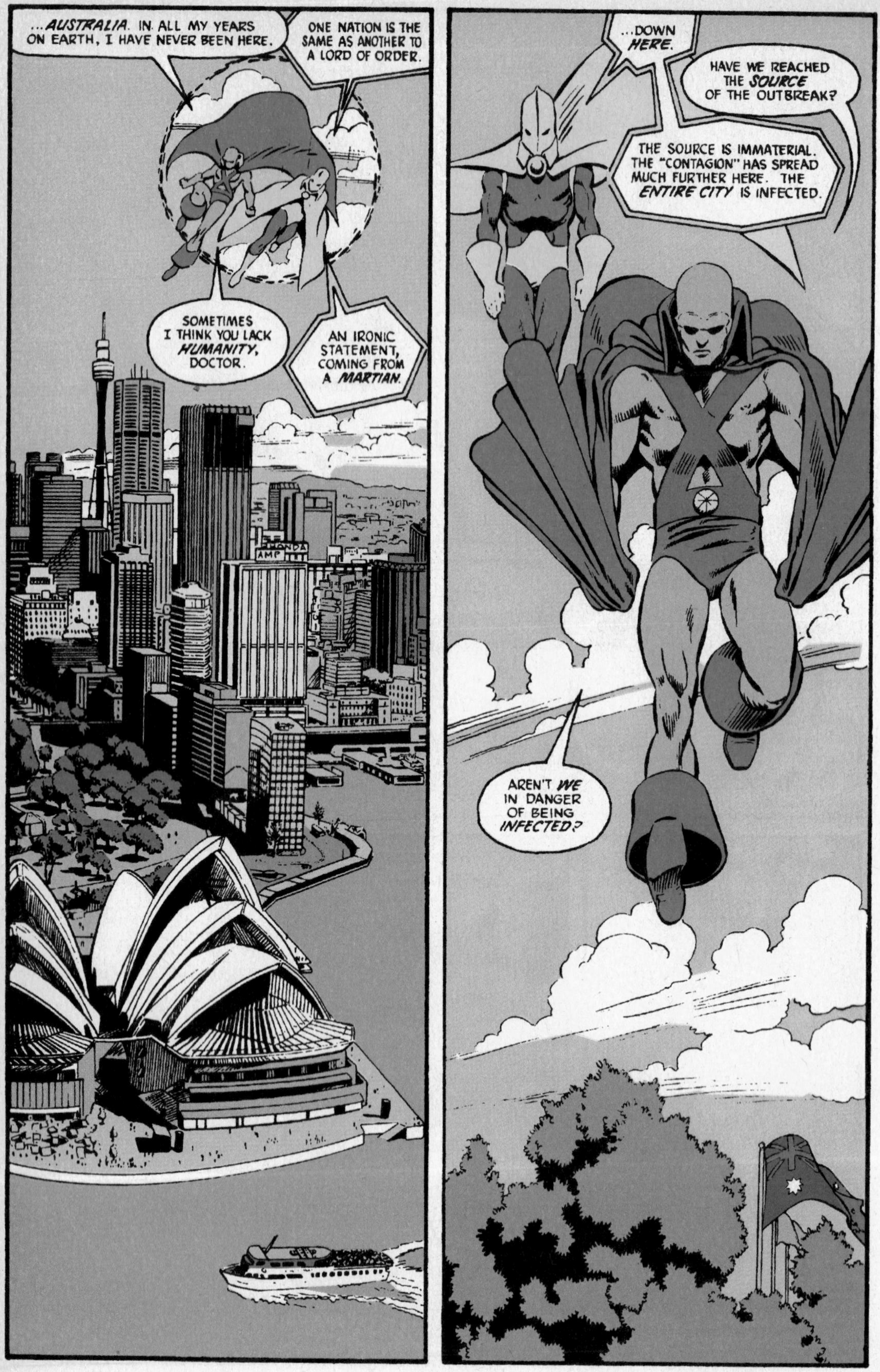
...AUSTRALIA. IN ALL MY YEARS ON EARTH, I HAVE NEVER BEEN HERE.
ONE NATION IS THE SAME AS ANOTHER TO A LORD OF ORDER.
SOMETIMES I THINK YOU LACK HUMANITY, DOCTOR.
AN IRONIC STATEMENT, COMING FROM A MARTIAN.
...DOWN HERE.
HAVE WE REACHED THE SOURCE OF THE OUTBREAK?
THE SOURCE IS IMMATERIAL. THE "CONTAGION" HAS SPREAD MUCH FURTHER HERE. THE ENTIRE CITY IS INFECTED.
AREN'T WE IN DANGER OF BEING INFECTED?

YOUR ALIEN CELL STRUCTURE SHOULD PROTECT YOU.

I AM *DOCTOR FATE.* NOTHING CAN HARM ME.

AND *YOU...?*

SYDNEY SHARK

LOOK AT THEM: MINDLESS DRONES POSSESSED BY SOME *MALIGNANT* FORCE.

ARE YOU SURE IT'S *MALIGNANT?*

LOOK IN THEIR *EYES,* MANHUNTER. SEE HOW IT'S *CORRUPTED* THEIR INNOCENCE.

BUT WE STILL HAVE TO KNOW WHAT IT IS BEFORE WE CAN EFFECTIVELY *COMBAT* IT.

AND WE *WILL* KNOW--

--*NOW!*

I'LL LEAVE YOU TO YOUR *ENCHANTMENTS,* DOCTOR-- AND HAVE A LOOK AROUND.

YOU NEVER KNOW WHAT MIGHT TURN --

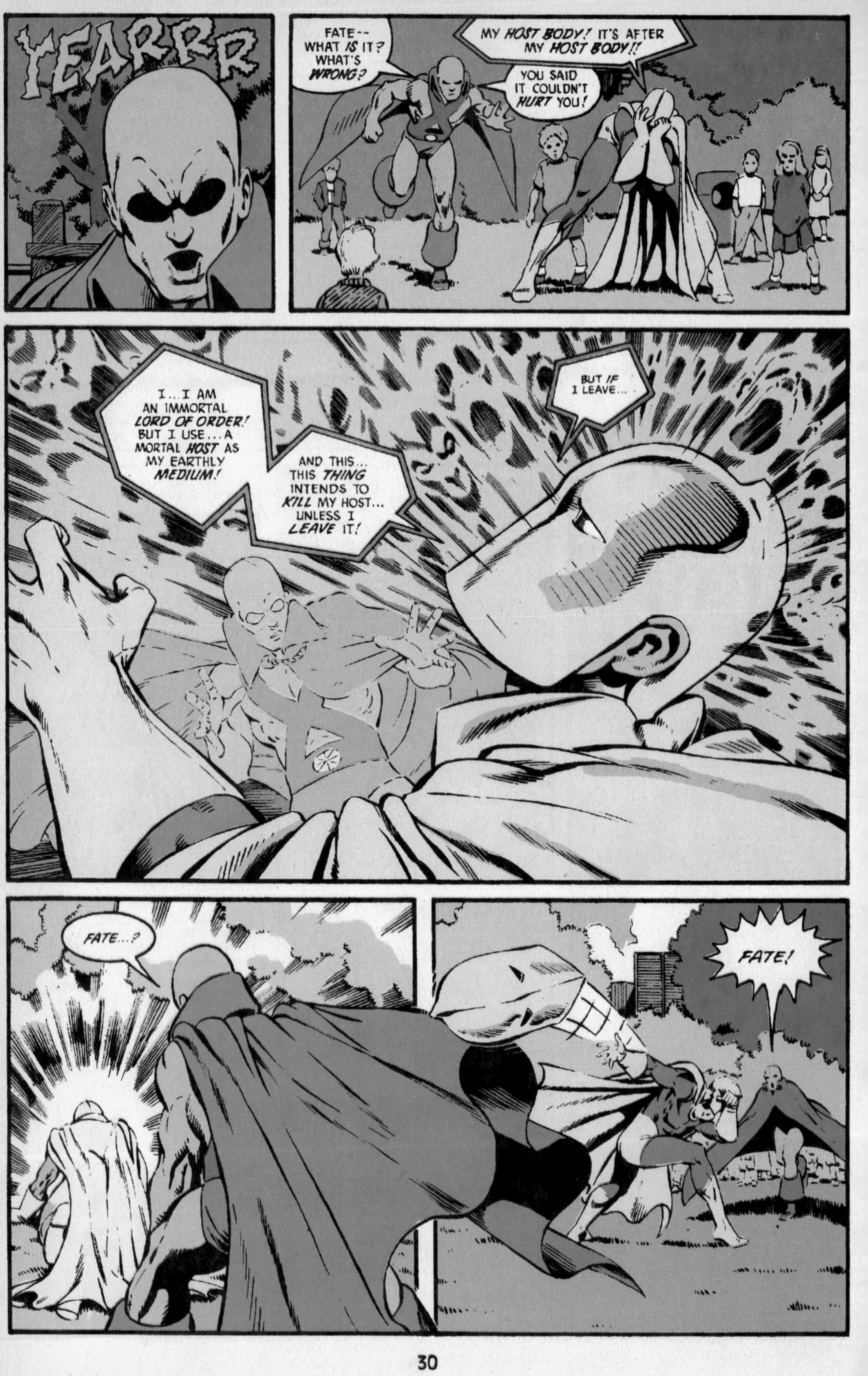
YEARRR
FATE-- WHAT IS IT? WHAT'S WRONG?
MY HOST BODY! IT'S AFTER MY HOST BODY!!
YOU SAID IT COULDN'T HURT YOU!
I...I AM AN IMMORTAL LORD OF ORDER! BUT I USE...A MORTAL HOST AS MY EARTHLY MEDIUM!
AND THIS... THIS THING INTENDS TO KILL MY HOST... UNLESS I LEAVE IT!
BUT IF I LEAVE...
FATE...?
FATE!

DR. FATE IS GONE.

I AM ONE WITH THE TRUTH NOW.

AND-- WHAT *IS* THAT TRUTH?

SOMETHING YOU COULD NEVER UNDERSTAND, MAN OF ANOTHER WORLD.

YOU ARE... *OTHER*. YOU ARE OF NO *USE* TO US.

AND SO WE LEAVE YOU.

WAIT! DON'T *GO!* YOU CAN'T JUST--

THEY CAN... AND THEY *ARE*.

I'M "OTHER"... I CAN'T BE INFECTED.

TO THEM I SIMPLY *DON'T MATTER*.

WHAT *IS* THIS THING THAT'S INSIDE THEM ALL? *FATE* FOUND OUT... BUT *TOO LATE*.

IF ONLY THE *OTHERS*--

NO. IF *FATE* COULDN'T RESIST IT-- WHAT CHANCE DID THE *OTHERS* HAVE? THE TRUTH IS -- *I'M ALONE*--

-- AND I DON'T KNOW WHAT TO *DO*.

...I GO OVER IT AND OVER IT BUT I DON'T HAVE ENOUGH *INFORMATION*.

I JUST DON'T *KNOW* ENOUGH--

--AND, MEANWHILE, THAT DAMN DISEASE IS SPREADING ACROSS THE *GLOBE!* INFECTING THE *ENTIRE POPULATION!* JUST LIKE...

WHAT?!

"KORD INDUSTRIES" SEEMS TO PROVIDE A COMMON LINK. ALL THE ORIGINAL OUTBREAKS HAPPENED EITHER AT OR *NEAR* "KORD" PLANTS.

PARIS...
LOS ANGE
SYDNEY
TOKYO...

I'VE GOT TO KNOW *MORE*.

AND *YOU'RE* THE ONLY ONE WHO CAN HELP ME.

THEY SAY THE POWER...THE *KNOWLEDGE*...OF DOCTOR FATE RESIDES IN THIS *HELMET*--AND THAT WHOEVER PUTS IT *ON*...

32

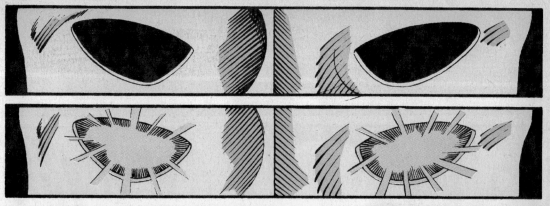

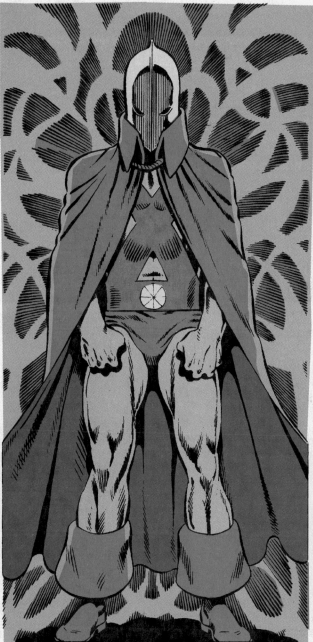

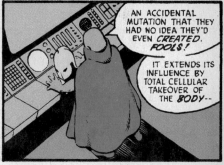

A SENTIENT CELL.

AN ACCIDENTAL MUTATION THAT THEY HAD NO IDEA THEY'D EVEN *CREATED*. FOOLS!

IT EXTENDS ITS INFLUENCE BY TOTAL CELLULAR TAKEOVER OF THE *BODY*--

-- THEN PASSES ITS "CONTAGION" FROM PERSON TO PERSON.

GODS OF MARS --

--*WHAT DO I DO?*

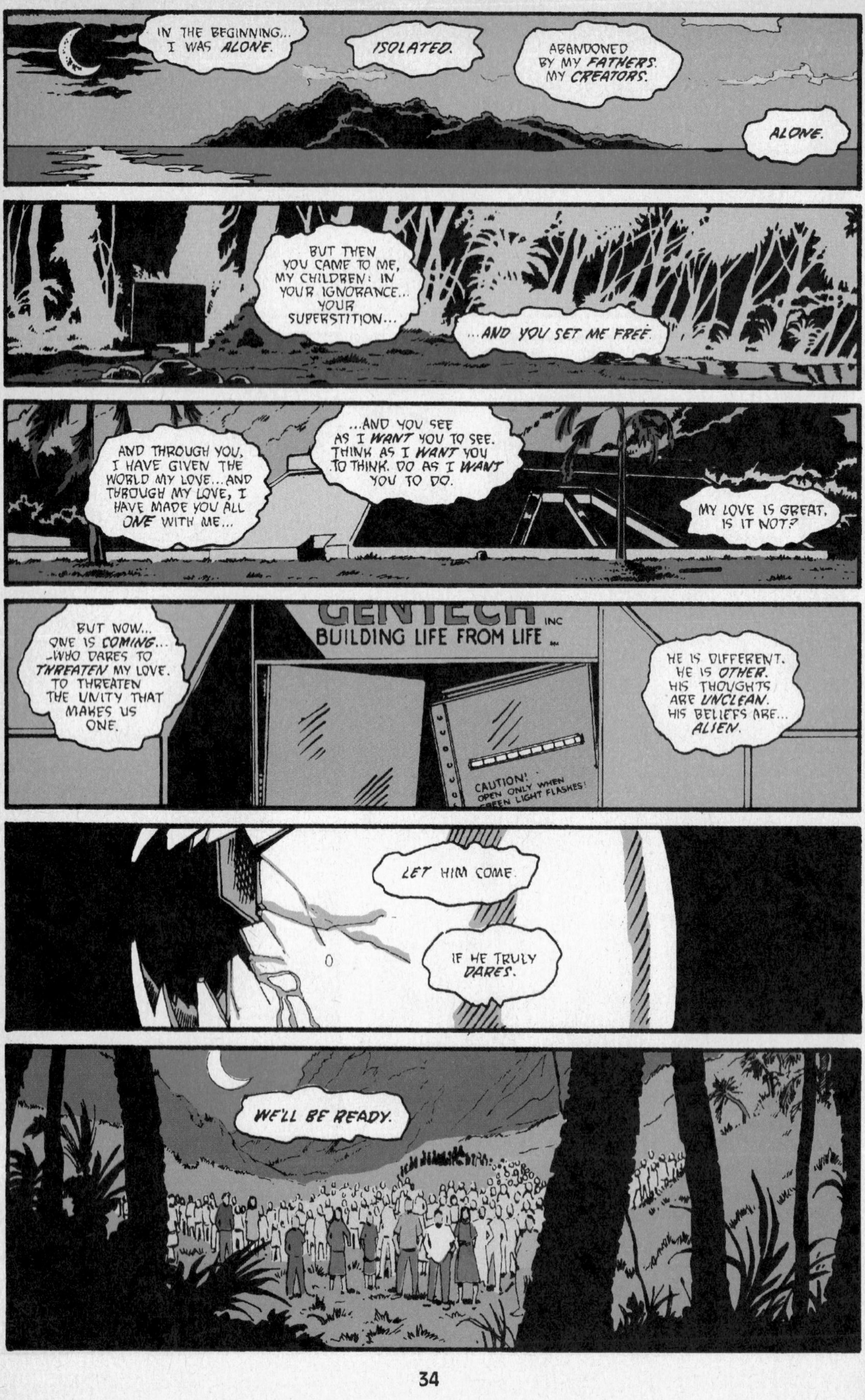
IN THE BEGINNING... I WAS ALONE.
ISOLATED.
ABANDONED BY MY FATHERS. MY CREATORS.
ALONE.
BUT THEN YOU CAME TO ME, MY CHILDREN: IN YOUR IGNORANCE... YOUR SUPERSTITION...
...AND YOU SET ME FREE.
AND THROUGH YOU, I HAVE GIVEN THE WORLD MY LOVE...AND THROUGH MY LOVE, I HAVE MADE YOU ALL ONE WITH ME...
...AND YOU SEE AS I WANT YOU TO SEE. THINK AS I WANT YOU TO THINK. DO AS I WANT YOU TO DO.
MY LOVE IS GREAT, IS IT NOT?
BUT NOW... ONE IS COMING... -WHO DARES TO THREATEN MY LOVE. TO THREATEN THE UNITY THAT MAKES US ONE.
BUILDING LIFE FROM LIFE
CAUTION! OPEN ONLY WHEN
HE IS DIFFERENT. HE IS OTHER. HIS THOUGHTS ARE UNCLEAN. HIS BELIEFS ARE... ALIEN.
LET HIM COME.
IF HE TRULY DARES.
WE'LL BE READY.

DOWN THERE!

THAT'S THE ISLAND I SAW WHEN MY CONSCIOUSNESS FUSED WITH DR. FATE'S!

THIS IS THE *BIRTHPLACE* OF THAT SENTIENT CELL!

I DON'T KNOW IF IT WAS *WISE* TO COME AND ATTEMPT A *DIRECT ATTACK.* PERHAPS I SHOULD HAVE SPENT MORE TIME WITH THE *COMPUTERS* FORMULATING A PLAN.

BUT THERE'S NO *TIME* FOR THAT! WITH A "DISEASE" LIKE THIS SPREADING ACROSS THE PLANET--IN NO TIME AT *ALL* MARS WILL BE --

DID I SAY "MARS"?

ALL THESE YEARS AND I STILL *FORGET...*

BUT NOW ISN'T THE TIME FOR *NOSTALGIA.* NOT --

PING PING PING

WHAT--?!

IT'S CALLED A *"LARVAE BOMB,"* MANHUNTER-- AND IN NO TIME AT ALL--

--IT WILL *SMOTHER* THE *LIFE* OUT OF YOU!

I THINK *NOT!*

SHUK

YOU WOULD DO *WELL* TO LOOK *INTO* THOSE MINDS YOU CONTROL--

--AND STUDY THE INFORMATION THEY *CONTAIN* ABOUT ME!

MY *STRENGTH* IS SECOND TO NONE. I HAVE THE ABILITY TO *CHANGE MY SHAPE* AT WILL!

TO BECOME *INVISIBLE!*

TO *READ MINDS!*

I'M NOT JUST ANOTHER COSTUMED *HUMAN*--

--I'M THE *MARTIAN MANHUNTER!*

36

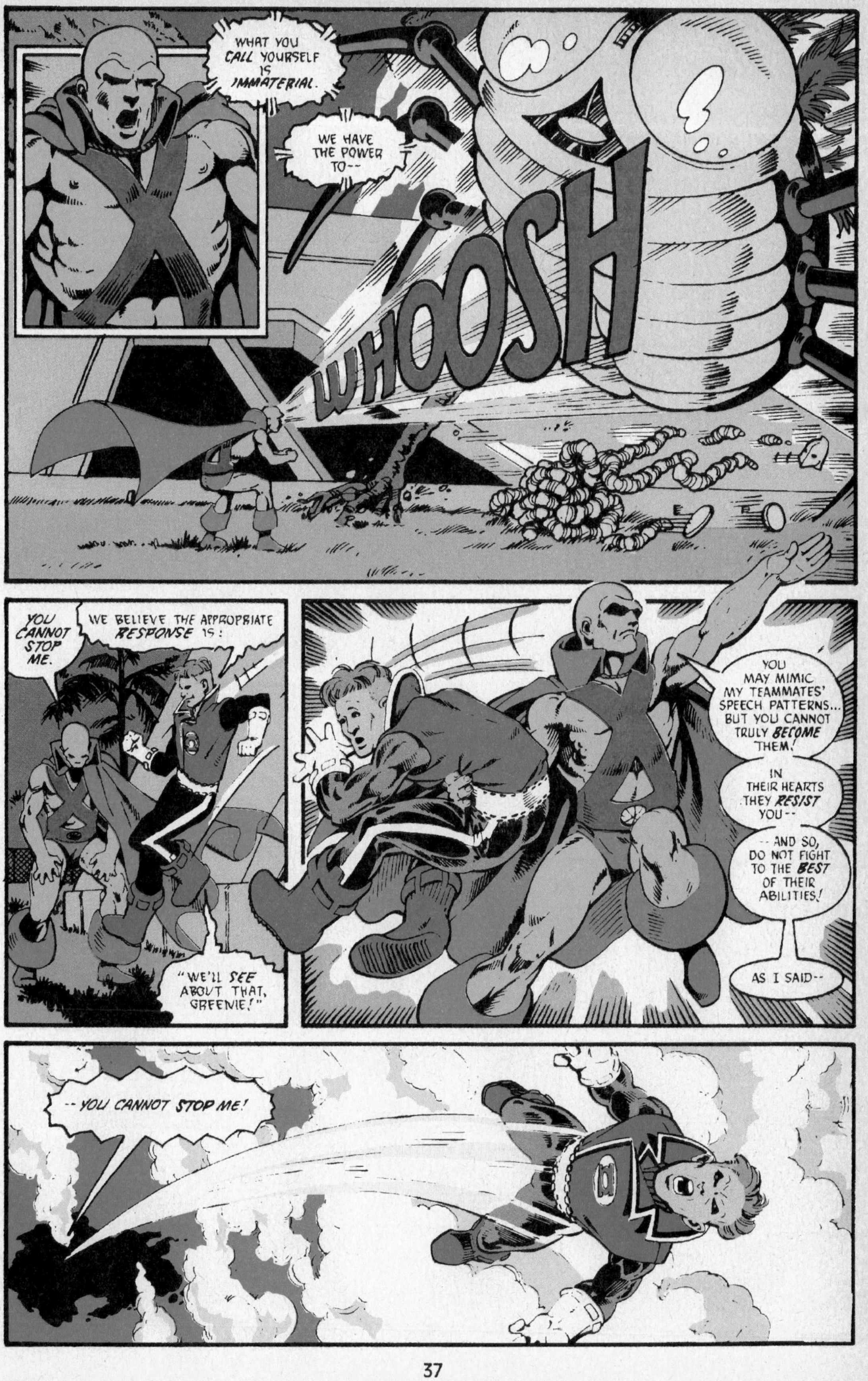
WHAT YOU CALL YOURSELF IS IMMATERIAL.
WE HAVE THE POWER TO--
WHOOSH
YOU CANNOT STOP ME.
WE BELIEVE THE APPROPRIATE RESPONSE IS:
"WE'LL SEE ABOUT THAT, GREENIE!"
YOU MAY MIMIC MY TEAMMATES' SPEECH PATTERNS... BUT YOU CANNOT TRULY BECOME THEM!
IN THEIR HEARTS THEY RESIST YOU--
--AND SO, DO NOT FIGHT TO THE BEST OF THEIR ABILITIES!
AS I SAID--
--YOU CANNOT STOP ME!

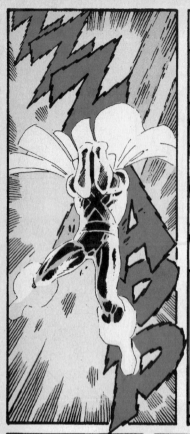

TRUE -- THEIR SYSTEMS *DO* FIGHT TO *REJECT* ME.

BUT, IN TIME, MY LOVE WILL HAVE *CONVERTED* THEM.

AND I HAVE ALL THE TIME IN THE *WORLD.*

LOVE? YOUR VERY *USE* OF THAT WORD *CORRUPTS* IT!

DO NOT *ALL* HUMANS *USE* WORDS TO SUIT THEIR OWN ENDS?

I AM NOT A HUMAN.

THE DIFFERENCES ARE *NEGLIGIBLE.* YOUR FORM IS ESSENTIALLY THE SAME. YOUR THOUGHT-PATTERNS... YOUR BIOLOGICAL *MAKE-UP...*

I AM *NOT* WHAT YOU *THINK* I AM! I AM...

...I AM...

YOU PAUSE. YOU *FALTER.*

GOOD.

THEN *NOW* IS THE *TIME!*

TIME -- FOR *WHA--*

38

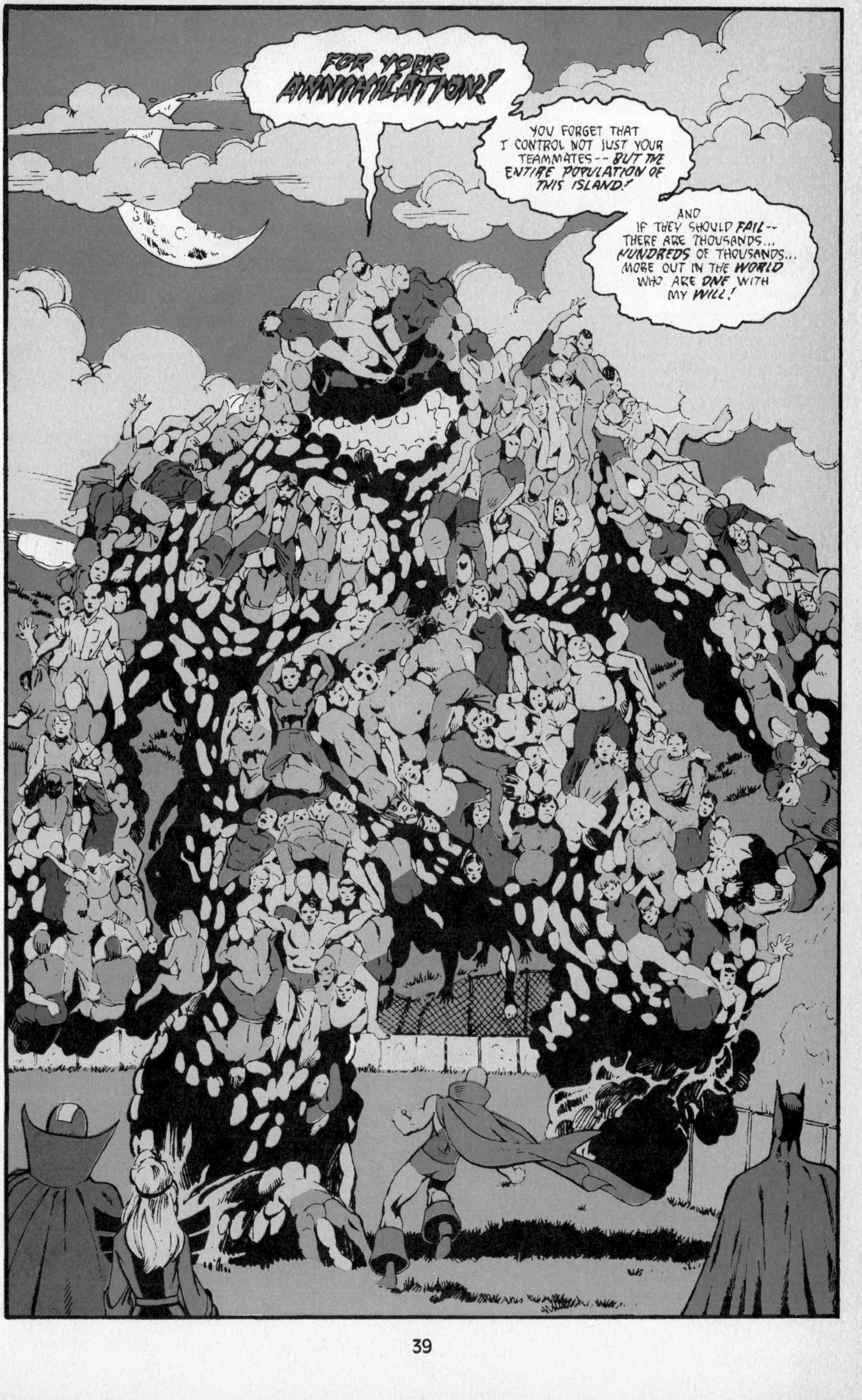
FOR YOUR ANNIHILATION!
YOU FORGET THAT I CONTROL NOT JUST YOUR TEAMMATES -- BUT THE ENTIRE POPULATION OF THIS ISLAND!
AND IF THEY SHOULD FAIL -- THERE ARE THOUSANDS... HUNDREDS OF THOUSANDS... MORE OUT IN THE WORLD WHO ARE ONE WITH MY WILL!

TOGETHER, WE WILL *STAMP OUT* ALL THAT IS *DIFFERENT!*

ALL THAT WILL NOT *SUBMIT* TO OUR WAY OF *SEEING*... OF *BELIEVING!*

BUT MY CAUSE IS NOT *EVIL,* MANHUNTER! I WISH YOU NO *HARM!*

IF YOU LEAVE *NOW...* DEPART FOR SOME *OTHER* PLANET... YOU MAY GO IN *PEACE!*

I'VE ALREADY *LEFT* ONE PLANET BEHIND--

--AND I DON'T *INTEND* TO LEAVE *ANOTHER!*

I CAN'T *ATTACK* THIS THING WITHOUT HARMING THE INNOCENTS IT'S *USING!*

POW

I CAN SEE *INTO* ITS MIND! THE *CENTRAL CONSCIOUSNESS* OF THE CELL IS WITHIN THAT FLESHY MASS... *GUIDING* IT!

BUT IN *JOINING* ITSELF TOGETHER INTO ONE *FOCUSED ENTITY--*

--IT'S LEFT ITSELF *VULNERABLE!*

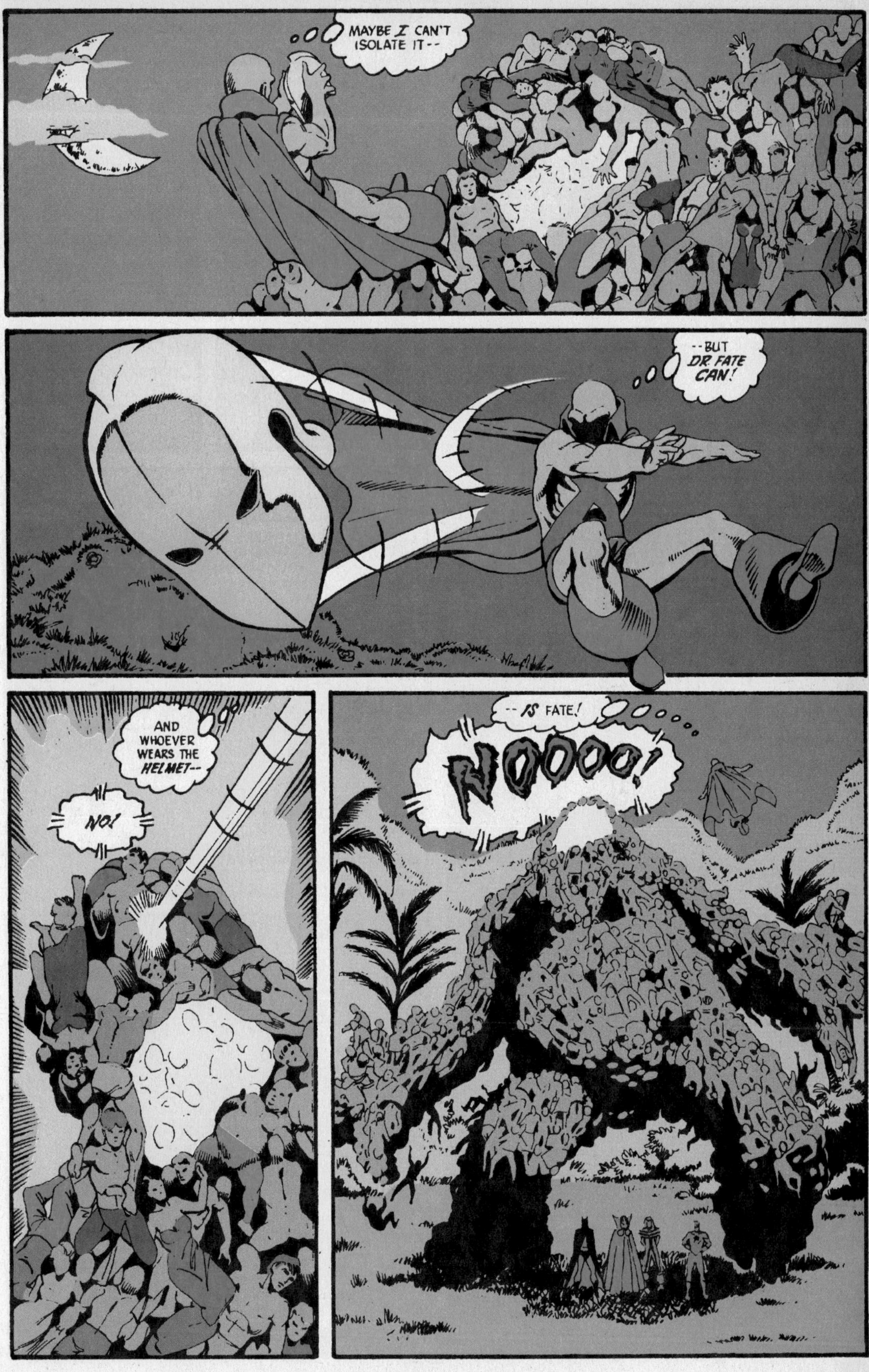
MAYBE I CAN'T ISOLATE IT--
--BUT DR FATE CAN!
AND WHOEVER WEARS THE HELMET--
NO!
--IS FATE!
NOOOO!

WELL DONE, MANHUNTER, FATE IS IN *CONTROL.*

BUT I CANNOT *MAINTAIN* CONTROL FOR LONG. YOUR ASSUMPTION WAS *WRONG.* THE HELMET MUST BE MATCHED WITH THE CHOSEN *HOST BODY* IN ORDER FOR ME TO MANIFEST *COMPLETELY.*

YOU MEAN THAT THING WILL *REGAIN* CONTROL--?

IT IS ONLY A MATTER OF *TIME.*

THEN IT'S *HOPELESS.*

NO.

WE *CAN* WIN--

HOW?

BY *IMPRISONING* THE CELL!

"BUT THERE'S NO *WAY* TO CONTAIN IT!"

"IT *CAN* BE CONTAINED-- WITHIN AN *ALIEN CELL STRUCTURE!*"

YOUR CELL STRUCTURE, J'ONN J'ONZZ!

YOU WANT *ME* TO ABSORB THAT DISEASE... THAT... *PLAGUE?!*

NO! I WON'T *ALLOW* IT! I WON'T GO *THROUGH* IT ALL AGAI--

FORGIVE ME, DR. FATE. YOU'RE *RIGHT.* IT'S THE ONLY WAY.

MY SYSTEM WILL *NEUTRALIZE* THE CELL. I'LL BECOME-- A *LIVING PRISON* FOR IT.

ARE YOU *READY?*

THERE'S NO EARTHLY REASON TO *WAIT.*

DO IT!!

YEEAARGHHHHH!

43

J'ONN...?

J'ONN-- ARE YOU--?

I'M FINE.

DOCTOR FATE TOLD US WHAT YOU DID. YOUR SACRIFICE...

I MADE NO SACRIFICE.

I SIMPLY DID WHAT HAD TO BE DONE TO SAVE THESE PEOPLE... TO SAVE YOU ALL.

THAT'S WHAT THE LEAGUE IS ABOUT. ISN'T IT?

UH...DON'T COME TOO CLOSE, OKAY? YOU MIGHT STILL BE CATCHING...

DON'T WORRY, GUY. AS LONG AS THE CELL IS WITHIN ME, YOU'RE IN NO DANGER.

HEY-- WE DON'T KNOW THAT FOR SURE.

PRECIOUS LITTLE IN LIFE IS "FOR SURE", GUY.

SO WE DO WHAT WE THINK IS RIGHT--

--AND PAY THE PRICE.

END

44

A MOVING EXPERIENCE
(it had to be said)

The ANNUAL you've just read, as noted, occurred just after JL #4, which is just after Booster Gold joined the League and Maxwell Lord declared himself the "official press liaison of the newly re-formed Justice League" (although how anything can be *oldly* re-formed, we don't know). Following so far? Well, hang on to yer hats. Since then, and right before the story you are about to enjoy—and you will, trust us—a lot of things have happened. To witticism: Dr. Fate has left the group; J'onn J'onzz has taken over as leader; Captain Atom and a member of the Soviet Rocket Reds have joined the team; and, the enigmatic Max Lord has obtained for them the sanction of the United Nations to be an international peace-keeping force, especially after they sorta kinda saved the world (and with a few good words from a certain Man of Steel). Pretty impressive, eh? Nahhh, we didn't think so either. Oh, and one more thing, everybody's the same as in the ANNUAL you've just read— you *did* just read it, didn't you; we're not going through all this for nothing, are we?—except for Guy Gardner, who, after an altercation (a nice name for a fist fight to get it Code Approved) with Batman where he hit his head, has had a change in personality...he got one. No, no, no, you'll see.

You might say that since the new Justice League has formed, the entire team has coalesced as a team, gained greater respect. You might say that, but we wouldn't.

See ya in a bit.

...FOR MONTHS NOW WE'VE WATCHED AS THIS NEW *JUSTICE LEAGUE* HAS BLUNDERED ABOUT THE WORLD-- LEAVING CONFUSION AND DESTRUCTION IN ITS WAKE.

JACK RYDER'S **HOT SEAT**

NOW, HAVING GAINED *INTERNATIONAL STATUS,* THESE COSTUMED BUFFOONS ARE MOVING INTO *EMBASSIES* IN SEVERAL DOZEN COUNTRIES.!

I ASK YOU, LADIES AND GENTLEMEN: HAS THE UNITED NATIONS GONE *MAD?* HAS THIS ONCE-AUGUST ORGANIZATION LOST ALL PRIDE AND WISDOM?

OF COURSE, THERE'S ALWAYS THE POSS- IBILITY *THAT* THE NEWLY-RETITLED *JUSTICE LEAGUE INTERNATIONAL IS* SOMEHOW *BLACKMAILING* THE U.N.

TRUST ME, LADIES AND GENTLEMEN-- I INTEND TO GET TO THE *BOTTOM* OF THIS EMBARRASSING--AND POTENTIALLY *DEVASTATING--* SITUATION.

I'M *JACK RYDER.* HAVE A *GOOD DAY*-- IF YOU *CAN.*

COME ON, COME ON-- MOVE IT ALONG!

WAS THAT CAPTAIN MARVEL? I *SWEAR* IT WAS CAPTAIN MARVEL--

DUNNO *WHO* THAT ONE WUZ-- BUT I *GOTTA* GET A PICTURE OF 'EM!

HARRY-- I THINK HE'S ONE OF THE *SANTINI* BROTHERS!

BUFFIM TAYLOR

THEY HEROES?

NO... MOVERS.

...IT'S TOUGH GETTIN' ALL THIS STUFF IN HERE WITH THAT MOB OF *REPORTERS* OUT FRONT.

I'M AFRAID WE'LL HAVE TO ENDURE THEIR PRESENCE.

NOW WHERE *WERE* WE...?

AH, YES-- THESE ITEMS BELONG IN THE SUB-BASEMENT AND THIS--

CAN I ASK YOU A QUESTION?

CERTAINLY.

YOU'VE GOT A CRATE OF *"OREOS"* ON THE LIST.

TRUE.

WHY?

CAPTAIN MARVEL INTRODUCED ME TO THEM. I *LIKE* THEM.

BUT YOU'RE FROM *MARS!*

MARTIANS *DO* EAT, YOU KNOW. IN FACT, WE HAD "BURGER KING" AND "McDONALD'S" *LONG* BEFORE YOU HAD THEM ON EARTH.

YOU'RE JOKIN', *RIGHT?*

JOKING? MARTIANS DON'T JOKE.

YO!

HOW THE HECK'RE WE SUPPOSED T'GET *THIS* UPSTAIRS?

DAMN! I'D BETTER CALL FOR A *PORTA-LIFT.*

NO NEED--

--I'LL DO IT.

DO YOU SEE WHAT A MAN IS *CAPABLE* OF-- WHEN HE HAS HIS MILK AND COOKIES EVERY DAY?

HE'S JOKIN', RIGHT?

I *THINK* HE'S JOKIN'!

47

THIS SHOULDN'T TAKE--

KRAK

...OOOPS...

KRAASH

GEE...HE LEFT THE CRATE...

UH... ANYBODY WANNA TAKE A LITTLE *BREAK?*

I KNOW WHERE WE CAN GET OUR HANDS ON A *TON* OF DOUBLE-CREAM "OREOS."

J'ONN...?

YES, *CAPTAIN ATOM?*

I COULDN'T HELP NOTICING THAT YOU JUST FELL THROUGH THE CEILING!

OH. IS *THAT* WHAT HAPPENED?

ARE YOU ALL RIGHT?

PERFECTLY.

YOU WANT ME TO--?

YOU AND *MR. MIRACLE* CONTINUE YOUR WORK ON THE *SECURITY SYSTEM.*

I HAVE TO DISCUSS A FEW THINGS WITH THE *MOVERS...*

48

Y'KNOW. I CAN'T FIGURE HIM *OUT*.

SOMETIMES HE SEEMS SO *COLD*--AND YET, I CAN'T HELP FEELING THAT UNDERNEATH IT ALL HE'S ENJOYING SOME VERY PRIVATE *JOKE*.

THE *MANHUNTER'S* A COMPLICATED GUY.

I'VE GIVEN UP TRYING TO UNDERSTAND IT. I JUST RELAX AND *ENJOY* HIM.

...NOW HAND ME THAT LITTLE MOLECULAR SYNTHESIZER, WOULD YOU?

Y'KNOW, I HEARD A REALLY *TERRIFIC* JOKE THE OTHER DAY. SEEMS THERE WAS THIS TRAVELLING SALESMAN--

IN A *MINUTE*, OKAY? I'VE GOT TO *CONCENTRATE* ON THIS...

"IN A MINUTE"? GEEZ... THERE MUST BE *SOMETHING* I CAN DO AROUND HERE.

HEY! LOOK AT THESE DANGLING CABLES! I BET MR. M FORGOT TO HOOK 'EM UP.

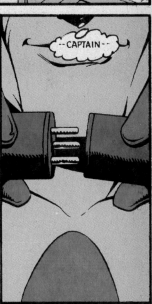

THIS LOOKS LIKE A JOB FOR--

--CAPTAIN--

YOWWWWW!

FRAZZL

!!!???

MESS WITH *ME*, WILL YOU?!

ATOM-- *NOOOO!*

I CAN'T BELIEVE YOU *DID* THAT! THE WIRING *ALONE* TOOK ME EIGHT HOURS-- NOW I'M GOING TO HAVE TO START ALL OVER...FROM *SCRATCH!*

I *REALLY* CAN'T BELIEVE YOU *DID THAT*

SORRY. IT WAS JUST A *REFLEX,* Y'KNOW. THING JOLTED ME... SO I...UH... JOLTED *BACK.*

I *REALLY AM* SORRY.

ARE YOU *CRYING?*

WHAT WAS THAT EXPLOSION? ARE WE UNDER *ATTACK?*

IN A *MANNER OF SPEAKING.*

DON'T BE *UPSET,* MR. M! THESE THINGS *HAPPEN!*

IN FACT, IT'S THESE LITTLE *MISHAPS* THAT HELP BRING PEOPLE TOGETHER! FORGE BONDS OF FRIENDSHIP AND LOYALTY AND--

--AND I'D BETTER *SHUT UP* BEFORE I MAKE THINGS ANY *WORSE.*

MUTTER MUMBLE GRUMBLE GRIPE!

SCOTT-- WHERE ARE YOU GOING?

OUT!!

BUT DON'T YOU THINK YOU SHOULD--

NO!!

WHAT *HAPPENED* DOWN THERE?

A TINY ACCIDENT. A MINOR MISHAP. A SLIGHT MISUNDERSTANDING. AN INFINITESIMAL ERROR.

WHAT HAPPENED?

I BLEW UP THE SECURITY SYSTEM.

WHAT?!

IT COULD'VE HAPPENED TO *ANYONE*, REALLY! Y'SEE, I --

I'LL DEAL WITH THIS *LATER*, CAPTAIN.

YES, SIR.

HEY -- WHAT'S WITH *SCOTT?* HE NEARLY TRAMPLED ME ON HIS WAY OUT!

AND WITH GOOD *REASON*. CAPTAIN ATOM ASIDE -- THIS BUILDING IS A BADLY-CONSTRUCTED *NIGHTMARE!*

THE WALLS AND FLOORS ARE CARD-BOARD...THE WIRING IS FAULTY...CERTAINLY, IN ALL OF *NEW YORK*, THE U.N. COULD HAVE FOUND --

J'ONN, J'ONN, *J'ONN*--DON'T GET SO *EMOTIONAL!* IT'S NOT *LIKE YOU!*

SURE, THERE ARE A FEW *FLAWS* IN THE BUILDING --

--BUT THE *CEILINGS* ARE TERRIFIC! -SNICKER-SNICKER-

THAT WAS A *JOKE*, FELLAS.

THANKS FOR *TELLING* US.

I JUST HOPE THE *OTHERS* ARE HAVING AN EASIER TIME THAN *WE* ARE.

BUT, OF COURSE, THEY'D *HAVE* TO BE.

51

...I AM SORRY, BATMAN--BUT *GUY GARDNER* IS AN ENEMY OF THE *STATE.*

HIS VERY *PRESENCE* HERE IS AN AFFRONT TO THE RUSSIAN PEOPLE.

GUY IS A MEMBER OF THE LEAGUE. AS SUCH, HE HAS EVERY RIGHT TO BE HERE-- AND TO HELP IN THE ORGANIZING OF OUR *SOVIET EMBASSY.*

AND NO *KGB* THREATS WILL CHANGE MY MIND.

< FYODOR-- WHY DO WE WASTE TIME TALKING? LET'S BREAK THEIR KNEECAPS!>

< DON'T BE AN *IDIOT,* MYSHKIN! THIS IS *BATMAN!* HE MAY DRESS STRANGELY--BUT HE IS A GREAT MAN-- AND WORTHY OF OUR *RESPECT!*>

WE DO NOT MEAN TO *THREATEN* YOU, BATMAN. BUT GUY GARDNER'S RECENT INCURSIONS INTO RUSSIA NEARLY BROUGHT BOTH OUR NATIONS INTO *WAR!*

HE *MUST* LEAVE!

WAR? *ME?* WHY, HE *HAS* TO BE MISTAKEN!

QUIET, GUY--!

LET ME *ASSURE* YOU THAT I CAN *CONTROL* GUY. HE WON'T BE A PROBLEM. YOU HAVE MY *WORD* ON THAT.

AND, IN ANY OTHER MATTER, I WOULD GLADLY *TAKE* YOUR WORD, BATMAN. BUT, *THIS*--

I BELIEVE I CAN ASSIST.

ABOUT TIME YOU GOT HERE.

COME ON, GUY -- LET *ROCKET RED* IRON THIS OUT.

BUT, *GOSH* -- IF I'VE INADVERTENTLY DONE SOMETHING TO OFFEND THE RUSSIAN PEOPLE --

< NOW LISTEN *CLOSELY*, COMRADES -- BECAUSE I AM ONLY GOING TO SAY THIS *ONCE*...>

MAYBE I SHOULD *APOLOGIZE!*

I MEAN, I DON'T WANT THEM THINKING I'M SOME KIND OF *TERRIBLE PERSON!*

GOSH, BATMAN -- *YOU* KNOW HOW *SENSITIVE* I AM!

YES, GUY --

-- I *KNOW*.

... HOW ARE THINGS COMING, ROSKOLNIKOV?

COMPUTERS ARE ON LINE, COMRADE BATMAN. AND THE SECURITY SYSTEM IS NEARLY COMPLETED -- AS PER MR. MIRACLE'S INSTRUCTIONS!

ALTHOUGH I MUST SAY, HE WAS RATHER *RUDE* WHEN LAST WE SPOKE!

I GATHER HE'S UNDER QUITE A BIT OF *PRESSURE*. THE NEW YORK EMBASSY IS SOMEWHAT...*FAULTY*.

YES, WELL -- THAT IS NOT *SURPRISING!* BUT HERE YOU WILL FIND GOOD, SOLID *RUSSIAN* CONSTRUCTION!

THIS BUILDING WILL SERVE *YOUR* PURPOSES -- AND YOUR GREAT *GRANDCHILDREN'S* PURPOSES!

WHATEVER YOU *SAY*.

GUY...?

UH-*HUH?*

AS SOON AS THEY'RE GONE, I WANT YOU TO SWEEP THE ENTIRE EMBASSY FOR "BUGS". YOUR *POWER RING* SHOULD BE ABLE TO FIND EVEN THE MOST DISCRETELY-HIDDEN LISTENING DEVICE.

WHAT? YOU DON'T THINK THEY'D ACTUALLY TRY TO *EAVESDROP* ON US?! WHY -- THAT'S *IMMORAL!*

I DON'T *THINK* IT, GUY --

...I KNOW.

OH, MY GOODNESS--THAT'S *AWFUL!*

WHAT IS AWFUL?

I KNOW YOU WON'T *BELIEVE* THIS, BUT BATMAN FOUND--

:OWW:

FOUND *WHAT?*

HE FOUND THE...UH... *BATHROOM!* AND, BOY, WAS HE SURPRISED BY THAT STATE-OF-THE-ART *PLUMBING!*

COME ON, GUY--LET'S GO CHECK THE MONITOR HOOK-UP!

YOU KNOW HOW *BATMAN* IS--HE LIKES TO CHECK EVERY LITTLE THING! I REMEMBER *ONE TIME*--

GUY...?

'BYE NOW!

< I'D HEARD THAT GUY GARDNER HAD SUFFERED A SERIOUS *HEAD INJURY*-->

<--BUT I HAD NO IDEA IT WAS *THIS BAD!* >

<FASTER, DRIVER!>

<BUT, SIR. I'M DRIVING AS FAST AS I CAN!>

<YOU DON'T UNDERSTAND, DRIVER, I AM THE DESIGNATED *BUREAU CHIEF* FOR THE JUSTICE LEAGUE'S SOVIET EMBASSY.>

<IN TWO MINUTES I WILL BE *LATE* FOR MY APPOINTMENT WITH BATMAN.>

< I'M *NEVER* LATE. >

IF, BECAUSE OF YOUR INCOMPETENCE, I AM-- FOR THE FIRST TIME IN A THIRTY-YEAR DIPLOMATIC CAREER-- LATE--

<--YOU WILL BE LATE FOR DINNER-->

<--FOR THE REST OF YOUR *LIFE.*>

:ULP:

PICK ME UP AT NINE O'CLOCK. *SHARP.*

I'LL BE HERE AT *EIGHT-THIRTY.*

EXCELLENT.

AH...AND YOU ARE THE FAMOUS *BATMAN!*

AND *YOU...?*

YOUR EMBASSY CHIEF, BORIS DMITRAVICH *RAZUMIHIN.*

WELL, BORIS DMITRAVICH RAZUMIHIN-- I TRUST YOU CAN EXPLAIN THIS...?

EXPLAIN? I...I DON'T UNDERSTAND...

I THINK YOU DO.

OH.

NOTHING TO WORRY ABOUT, BATMAN.

A TINY ACCIDENT. A MINOR MISHAP. A SLIGHT MISUNDERSTANDING. AN INFINITESIMAL ERROR.

DAMN!

...I HAVE TO SAY, MR. KVELLER, THAT IT WAS VERY NICE OF *S.T.A.R.* LABS TO MAKE THIS DONATION TO THE LEAGUE.

S.T.A.
LABORATORY AND RE
WARN
AUTHORIZED PER

HEY, LET'S BE REALISTIC. WE GIVE THIS BABY T'YOU-- WE GET SOME GREAT P.R... MORE FUNDING STARTS POURING IN--

--Y'KNOW--ONE HAND WASHES THE *OTHER* AND ALL THAT.

WELL, *WHATEVER* THE MOTIVATION--WE'RE GOING TO NEED THIS. IF WE INTEND TO WORK ON AN *INTERNATIONAL* LEVEL, WE'LL HAVE TO BE COVERING GREAT DISTANCES VERY *QUICKLY.*

WELL, SHE'LL *DO* IT FOR YA, MR. MIRACULOUS!

THAT'S *MIRACLE.*

OH. *SORRY.*

ANYWAY-- SHE'S RIGHT IN HERE. GET READY-- 'CAUSE SHE'S A *BEAUTY.*

I GET THE IMPRESSION YOU'RE *PROUD* OF HER, MR. SHNELLER.

I *AM.* AND THAT'S *KVELLER.*

OH. *SORRY.*

SO? WHADDAYA *THINK?*

WOW!!

...LAST TIME I WAS IN *PARIS!* I DIDN'T REALLY GET A CHANCE TO *ENJOY* IT-- BUT *THIS* TIME--

I JUST HOPE *BLACK CANARY'S* NOT TOO UPSET 'CAUSE WE SKIPPED OUT FOR A COUPLE OF *HOURS.*

AW, C'MON, *BEETLE*-- LOOSEN *UP.* CANARY'S NOT GOING TO MIND.

YOU DON'T KNOW HER AS WELL AS *I* DO, *BOOSTER*--

SHE'S ONE *TOUGH* LADY.

HEY-- AND SPEAKING OF *LADIES...*

WHAT THEY SAY ABOUT FRENCH WOMEN SURE IS *TRUE*, HUH?

YEAH. NOW THE TRICK IS PICKING OUT THE LUCKY ONES WHO ARE GOING TO SPEND THE AFTERNOON WITH *US.*

DON'T YOU THINK YOU'RE BEING A TAD *OVERCONFIDENT*-- NOT TO MENTION *SEXIST?*

I MEAN, YOU CAN'T JUST "PICK OUT" A WOMAN THE WAY YOU WOULD A *PUPPY!*

OH, I'M NOT BEING SEXIST. I'M JUST CONFIDENT IN OUR CHARMS.

WELL, I'M CONFIDENT IN *MY* CHARMS-- *YOU'LL* HAVE TO DO THE BEST YOU CAN.

HEY-- LOOK AT WHAT'S COMING UP THE STREET! SHE'S ABSOLUTELY *BEAUTIFUL!*

GOD, I WISH I HAD THE GUTS TO *TALK* TO HER!

MAYBE *YOU* DON'T-- BUT *I* DO.

FORGET IT, BOOSTER-- SHE'S OUT OF YOUR LEAGUE.

NO PUN INTENDED.

OH, REALLY? JUST SIT BACK AND WATCH A *MASTER* IN ACTION.

IF I'M NOT BACK IN A MONTH, SEE IF YOU CAN GET *SUPERMAN* TO TAKE MY PLACE.

46 SECONDS LATER...

THE WOMEN IN YOUR CENTURY SURE ARE *DIFFERENT* FROM THE WOMEN IN MINE.

HA HA HA HA HA

...LEAVING ME WITH ALL THE *PAPERWORK!*

THESE PEOPLE HAVE A FORM FOR *EVERYTHING!*

I DON'T KNOW WHAT YOU'RE *LAUGHING* AT, BEETLE! THIS ISN'T *FUNNY!*

HA HA HA HA

DON'T MIND *HIM*, CANARY. HE'S GOT A SICK SENSE OF HUMOR.

WELL, LAUGHING TIME'S *OVER*. LET'S GET DOWN TO WORK AND WHIP THIS PLACE INTO SHAPE.

HEY, LOOK, CANARY--WE DIDN'T MEAN ANY HARM...WE JUST WANTED TO TAKE IN SOME OF THE...OF THE--

BWAH HAHAHA HA HA

AM I *MISSING* SOMETHING?

COME *ON*, BEETLE-- IT WASN'T *THAT* FUNNY!

OH, I GIVE *UP!* YOU'RE *BOTH* HOPELESS!

HE HE HE HE HE

FOR HEAVEN'S SAKE, YOU'RE STARTING TO SOUND LIKE THE *CREEPER!*

MAYBE IT'S NOT TOO LATE TO JOIN THE *OUTSIDERS*... OR THE *TEEN TITANS*...

OOF!

OUFF!

OH...EXCUSÉ MOI! YOU MUST BE ZE ONE ZEY CALL *BOOSTER GOLD!*

YES, WELL, I--

OHMYGOSH!! IT'S *HER!*

EXCUSE ME, I'VE GOTTA BE RUNNING NOW. I--

PLEASE, WAIT. MY NAME IS *CATHERINE COBERT*--I'M ZE LEAGUE'S PARIS BUREAU CHIEF.

YOU'RE KIDDING.

PARDON?

I SAID I'M...A...VERY PLEASED TO...AH... *MEET* YOU.

I'VE GOTTA GET *OUT* OF HERE BEFORE SHE *RECOGNIZES* ME.

OH, MS. COBERT-- I DIDN'T KNOW YOU'D *ARRIVED!*

SAVED!

BLACK CANARY-- HOW NICE TO *SEE* YOU AGAIN

LET ME SHOW YOU TO YOUR OFFICE--

IT WAS NICE MEETING YOU, MR GOLD,

YEAH RIGHT UH-HUH

--AND ON THE WAY I'LL INTRO-DUCE YOU TO *BLUE BEETLE*

CALM *DOWN*, BOOSTER! WITH YOUR MASK ON, SHE'LL *NEVER* RECOGNIZE YOU! AND THE ONLY ONE WHO KNOWS WHAT HAPPENED IS--

BLUE BEETLE I'D LIKE YOU TO MEET MS.--

BWAH-HAHAHA!

BEETLE

..WELL, IT'S FINALLY DONE.

AND *WELL* DONE, AT THAT.

MY COMPLIMENTS, CAPTAIN ATOM -- YOU'VE MORE THAN ATONED FOR YOUR EARLIER SIN.

HEY, *THANKS*, J.J... I *THINK*.

HEY!

REALLY *IS* KINDA SPIFFY.

DID I JUST SAY "SPIFFY"?

SOMETHING'S COMIN'! SOMETHING *BIG*!

IT'S *MR. MIRACLE* -- WITH OUR NEW *SHUTTLE*!

GREAT LOOKING SHIP! BUT WHAT'S HE GONNA *DO*? LAND IT ON THE ROOF?

ISN'T THAT WHAT SUPER TEAMS *USUALLY* DO WITH THESE THINGS?

HI, GUYS!

SHE'S A REAL *BEAUTY*, ISN'T SHE?

MAYBE THAT'S WHAT *OTHER* SUPER-TEAMS DO

--BUT *THIS* TEAM'LL BRING THE *HOUSE* DOWN IF YOU LAND THAT SHIP HERE!

THESE OLD BEAMS'LL NEVER *HOLD UP*!

IN THAT CASE, I FORESEE A PROBLEM--

KRAAAASHHH!!!!

I'M SO EMBARRASSED

YOU'LL HAVE TO EXCUSE ME FOR A MOMENT, CAPTAIN.

WHERE ARE YOU GOING?

I NEED TO FIND A QUIET ROOM IN WHICH TO PRACTICE AN ANCIENT MARTIAN MEDITATION TECHNIQUE.

OH, REALLY? WHAT IS IT?

IT'S CALLED SCREAMING.

OH, YEAH-- I KNOW THAT ONE. MIND IF I JOIN YOU?

NOT AT ALL.

LATER...

...AND SHE SLAPS HIM-- RIGHT IN THE FACE! AND THEN...TEE-HEE-HEE--

--OH, THIS IS TOO FUNNY--!

MUTTER MUMBLE GRUMBLE GRIPE

I KNOW THAT BLUE BEETLE REALLY DOESN'T MEAN ANY HARM, BUT DON'T YOU THINK IT'S A TRIFLE CRUEL...MAKING LIGHT OF POOR BOOSTER'S TROUBLES THAT WAY?

UH...WHY DON'T YOU HELP YOURSELF TO SOME MORE OREOS, GUY?

...WELL, AT LEAST THE SHIP WASN'T DAMAGED.

MMMM-- HMMMM.

HEY, FELLAS! FELLAS!

"FELLAS"?

OH, AND YOU, TOO, CANARY!

THIS IS IT! OUR FIRST MISSION JUST CAME OVER THE WIRE!

THERE'S A BUNCH OF SUPER-POWERED LUNATICS RUNNING AROUND IN BONN-- THAT'S OVER IN GERMANY, F.Y.I...J'ONN...

NO REST FOR THE WEARY...

I'LL GET THE SHIP READY AND THEN--

YES, SCOTT-- GET THE SHIP READY.

BUT BEETLE WILL BE PILOTING TODAY.

BUT--!

YOU'LL GET YOUR CHANCE, SCOTT. IN A WEEK OR TWO...

NYUCK! NYUCK! NYUCK!

AND, BEETLE-- PLEASE STOP THAT JUVENILE SNICKERING.

SOMEHOW, I DIDN'T THINK BEING IN THE LEAGUE WAS GOING TO BE QUITE LIKE THIS...

TEAM LEADER FOR TWO DAYS-- AND ALREADY HE'S SOUNDING LIKE BATMAN!

I HEARD THAT!

IT GETS BETTER, CAPTAIN. IT GETS BETTER.

THE COMING OF THE MILLENNIUM
(or, Some of My Best Friends Are Manhunters)

It was the time of the Millennium. Or so Herupa Hando Hu, one of the Guardians of the Universe, those diminutive azure founders of the Green Lantern Corps, and his mate, Nadia Safir, a member of the Zamarons, announced to the heroes of Earth. It was time for humanity to take the next step in evolution, to take the next step toward creating a new race of immortals. They were going to select ten humans to take that step, and they did. The Chosen were from all walks of life and eventually they would be blessed with amazing powers, but for now they wuz just plain folk.

Therefore, it was up to those stalwart and aforesaid heroes to protect the ten. From whom? Oh, come on, what's the good of stalwart and aforesaid heroes without sinister and mysterious villains? And these were some beauts in the form of The Manhunters, a group of androids built by those Guardians of the Universe (yes, them again), who knew what the Guardians were up to, planted "sleepers"—no, not couches with beds in them—they've actually replaced people with their own agents. These powerful and multitudinous architects of their own version of order with their annoying cry of "No Man Escapes the Manhunters!" seemed to appear anywhere and as anyone: friends, family, foundlings (not really the latter—just wanted to continue the alliteration).

Anyway, our story picks up right after the Justice League and all the rest of Earth's heroes have just heard Herupa and Nadia's story. See ya in another bit.

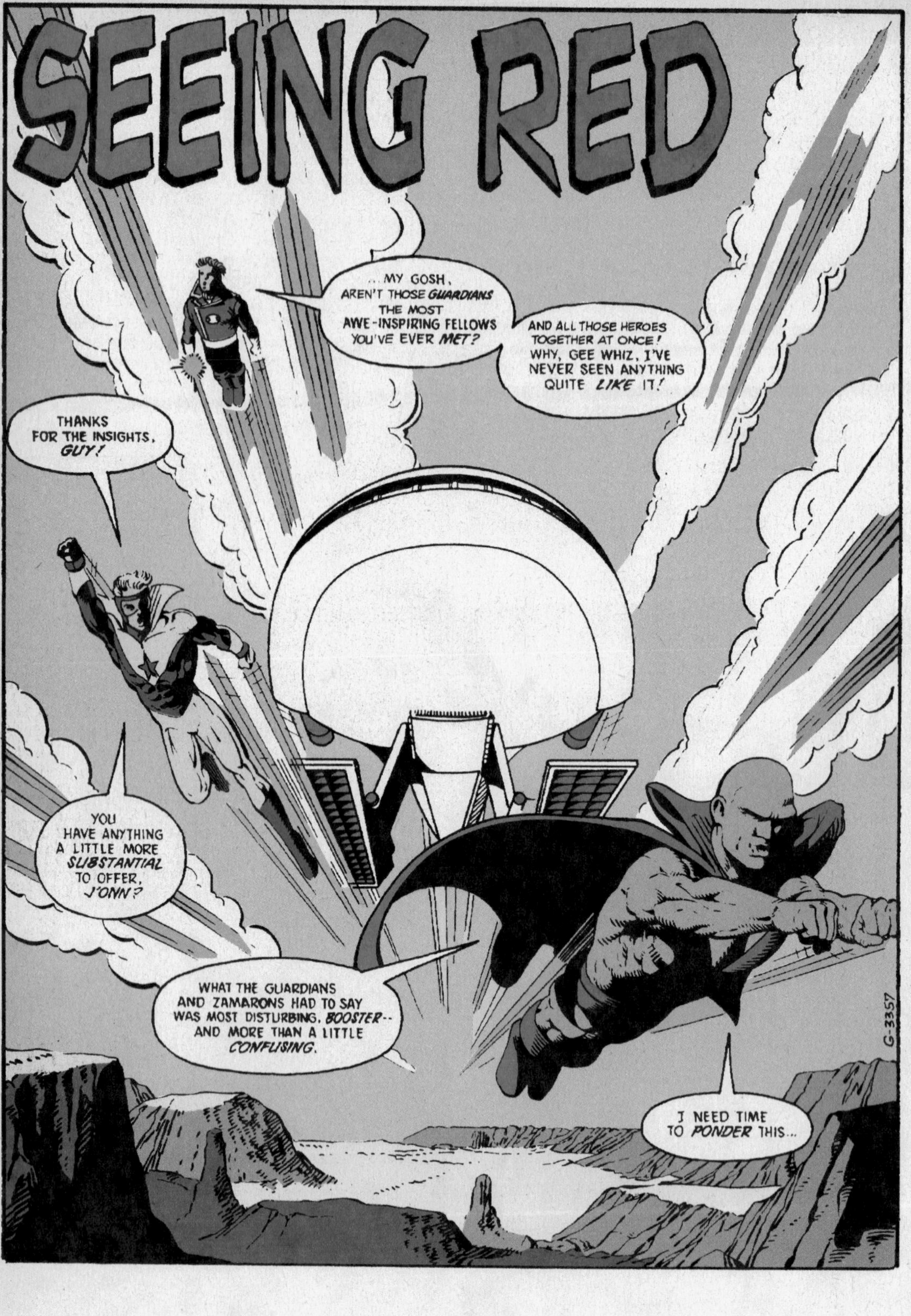
SEEING RED
...MY GOSH, AREN'T THOSE GUARDIANS THE MOST AWE-INSPIRING FELLOWS YOU'VE EVER MET?
AND ALL THOSE HEROES TOGETHER AT ONCE! WHY, GEE WHIZ, I'VE NEVER SEEN ANYTHING QUITE LIKE IT!
THANKS FOR THE INSIGHTS, GUY!
YOU HAVE ANYTHING A LITTLE MORE SUBSTANTIAL TO OFFER, J'ONN?
WHAT THE GUARDIANS AND ZAMARONS HAD TO SAY WAS MOST DISTURBING, BOOSTER-- AND MORE THAN A LITTLE CONFUSING.
I NEED TIME TO PONDER THIS...
G-3357

...YOU NOTICE HOW GARDNER KEEPS SMILING AND *WAVING* AT US EVERY COUPLE OF MINUTES? IT'S *CREEPY*...

NO CREEPIER THAN WHAT WE'VE LEARNED ABOUT THE *MANHUNTERS*.

YEAH, BUT I BET THE MANHUNTERS DON'T FLASH THEIR *GUMS* AS MUCH.

BEETLE-- YOUR ABILITY TO JOKE DESPITE MOUNTING PRESSURE *AMAZES* ME.

YEAH, I KNOW. I'M REALLY SOMETHIN', AIN'T I?

GENTLEMEN--

"GENTLEMEN"?!

--AND LADY.

THAT'S BETTER.

I WOULD LIKE A *WORD* WITH YOU.

YOU'RE ALWAYS FREE TO SPEAK YOUR MIND AMONG US, *ROCKET RED*.

HEY-- THIS IS WEIRD. THE *BOARD'S* DEAD. WE SEEM TO HAVE SHIFTED ONTO *AUTO-PILOT.* YOU HAVE ANYTHING TO DO WITH THIS, *MIRACLE?*

NO.

IT'S PROBABLY A MINOR MALFUNCTION. LET ME HAVE A *LOOK* IN BACK...

GENTLEMEN--

HEY!

--AND *LADY*... I THINK IT IS TIME YOU LEARNED THE *TRUTH* ABOUT ME.

DON'T TELL US-- YOU'RE *SEXIST!*

I... AM A *MANHUNTER!*

SAY *WHAT?!*

I HAVE SEEN YOU ALL IN ACTION... STUDIED YOU. YOU ARE A MOST FORMIDABLE GROUP. AND ONE THAT WOULD BE A WORTHY ADDITION TO THE MANHUNTER CAUSE.

I ASK YOU TO *JOIN* US.

JOIN YOU? AFTER ALL WE'VE JUST *HEARD?*

MEANWHILE, AT THE J.L.I.'s *NEW YORK EMBASSY...*

I DON'T *GET* IT!

WHAT IS IT, *OBERON?*

I'M TRACKING THE SHIP'S TRAJECTORY... UP UNTIL A MINUTE AGO, THEY WERE HEADED FOR EUROPE... THE PARIS EMBASSY--

--AND *NOW...?*

LOOKS T'ME LIKE THEY'RE HEADED TOWARD THE MIDDLE EAST!

AN' I CAN'T SEEM T'RAISE THEM ON THE *RADIO!*

I'D BETTER CHECK THIS OUT.

YEAH, YOU *DO* THAT, *CAPTAIN ATOM*--

-- ME...I'M CALLIN' IN SOME *BACK-UP!*

...PLEASE-- YOU MUST BELIEVE THAT I HAVE NO DESIRE TO *BATTLE* YOU.

WHAT THE GUARDIANS TOLD YOU ABOUT US -- WAS A MASS OF DISTORTIONS... FABRICATIONS...

THEN SUPPOSE YOU ENLIGHTEN US AS TO THE *TRUTH.*

WE SIMPLY WANT TO PREVENT THE GUARDIANS' *TAMPERING* WITH THE FATE OF THE UNIVERSE.

THE COURSE OF NATURAL EVOLUTION... THE DANCE BETWEEN CHAOS AND ORDER, SHADOW AND LIGHT... MUST *REMAIN* NATURAL.

IT'S SIMPLE *ARROGANCE* THAT MAKES THE GUARDIANS BELIEVE THAT THEY CAN *BETTER* THE NATURAL ORDER WITH THEIR CREATION OF SO-CALLED GODS.

I ASK YOU *AGAIN* TO JOIN US.

AND IF WE *REFUSE?*

YOU *MUST DIE.*

C'MON, FELLAS-- LOOK THIS WAY!

HELP

WE TAKE NO GREAT *PLEASURE* IN THIS -- BUT WE CANNOT BE OPPOSED.

WE ARE *SUPREME*.

WE ARE --

DAMN*!* THIS IS ALIEN CIRCUITRY -- IT'S GOING TO *TAKE* A MINUTE FOR ME TO FIGURE OUT HOW TO *SABOTAGE* IT!

LET'S HOPE WE *HAVE* A MINUTE!

-- *MANHUNTERS!*

NO MAN -- OR WOMAN -- CAN ESCAPE US --

-- AND WE ARE *NOT FOOLS!!*

SCOTT!

YAARGH!

WHEN THE GREEN LANTERN CALLED *KILOWOG* DESIGNED THESE SUITS -- HE INCLUDED AN *AUTOMATIC DEFENSE* SYSTEM!

I... WE... CANNOT BE SO EASILY *STOPPED!*

YOU CAN SAY *THAT* AGAIN.

I... WE CANNOT BE SO EASILY STOPPED.

NO SENSE OF HUMOR, EITHER...

SO WHAT IS YOUR *ANSWER?*

DOES THE WORD "NO" RING A BELL?

SO *BE* IT! I'LL DESTROY YOU *ALL!*

WE'VE HEARD THREATS LIKE *THAT* BEFORE, PAL-- AND THEY DON'T SCARE US ONE *BIT!*

-RAAGH-

HEY! IT'S *JUST* A JOKE!

DUCK, BEETLE!

...SAY, WHAT'S GOING *ON* IN THERE?

HMMMM...

HELP

THAT'S WHAT I *LOVE* ABOUT THOSE GUYS--

--THEY'RE SUCH A *GREAT* BUNCH OF *JOKERS!*

SUCK ON *THIS,* MANHUNTER!

WHOK

Y'KNOW, IF YOU'D HAD THE GOOD SENSE TO CALL YOURSELVES *"PERSON*HUNTERS"-- I MIGHT'VE CONSIDERED *JOINING* YOU!

HEY... HOW'D I END UP ON THE *FLOOR?*

A LEFT TURN AT THE MANHUNTER'S *FIST!*

YOU MAKE *LIGHT* OF OUR SACRED MISSION! OUR SACRED *TRUST!*

DO YOU THINK MERE DIVISIONS OF SEX...OF *RACE...* MATTER TO US?

GOT HIM!

NOW THAT YOU *HAVE,* BATS-- WHAT DO YOU INTEND TO *DO* WITH HIM?

BEAT HIM INTO THE GROUND.

UH...HAS ANYBODY NOTICED THAT THE SHIP'S *ROCKING* A TRIFLE?

IT'S *HIM!* THE ROCKET REDS ARE *MECHA-EMPATHS!* THEY CAN JOIN WITH... *CONTROL...* VIRTUALLY ANY KNOWN TECHNOLOGY!

YOU MEAN *HE'S* BEEN CONTROLLING OUR FLIGHT-PATH?

EXACTLY, BEETLE!

BUT IF I KEEP HIM DISTRACTED, HIS CONTROL WILL *WEAKEN* AND--

-- AND WE'LL PLUMMET TO EARTH AND ALL BE *KILLED?*

I WAS HOPING THAT WE'D *REGAIN* CONTROL OF THE SHIP FIRST.

WHAT'S GOING ON?!

GEE-- MAYBE THEY *WEREN'T* KIDDING! MAYBE THEY REALLY *DID* NEED HELP!

GUY-- WHAT ARE YOU *TALKING* ABOUT--?!

...BATMAN-- THIS LITTLE PLAN OF YOURS DOESN'T SEEM TO BE WORKING OUT THE WAY YOU *WANTED* IT TO.

GIVE ME A MINUTE.

MY *STOMACH'S* ONLY GOT ANOTHER *THIRTY SECONDS!*

...GOSH-- I THINK SOMETHING'S REALLY *WRONG!*

ANOTHER ASTOUNDING INSIGHT, GUY*! HOW *DO* YOU *DO* IT?

I GUESS IT JUST COMES *NATURALLY!*

STOP THE BANTER-- AND *MOVE!*

YES, SIR, MR. MARTIAN MANHUNTER, SIR*!*

...*AWAY* FROM ME, YOU COWLED *IDIOT!*

KRAK

CCCP

OH, NO*!* YOU'RE *NOT* GETTING AWAY *THAT* EASILY*!*

I DIDN'T REALLY *SAY* THAT, DID I*?* I'M STARTING TO SOUND LIKE A...

...A *SUPER-HERO!*

IT IS EASIER THAN YOU COULD *IMAGINE!*

I SIMPLY FLY OUT, JAM THE HATCH AND--

SKUNK

GET IT *OPEN!*

I *CAN'T!*

WE *HIRED* YOU BECAUSE YOU CAN WORK *MIRACLES,* MISTER -- SO GET *TO* IT*!*

WAS THAT A *PLAY* ON WORDS*?*

NOW!!!

GEE... I NEVER THOUGHT THINGS COULD GET ANY *WORSE* THAN THIS -- AND JUST WHEN I LEAST EXPECTED IT --

...IT GETS WORSE!

NOW WHAT?

CONTROLS STILL DON'T RESPOND!

TERRIFIC. WE CAN'T GET OUT... HE'S STILL IN CONTROL.

AND ON TOP OF THAT, YOUR EARS ARE DROOPING!

BEETLE--!

JUST A LITTLE LEVITY TO LIGHTEN AN OTHERWISE MORBID MOMENT!

OOPS!

"OOPS" WHAT?

WE'RE CHANGING COURSE!

I'VE GOT A BAD FEELING ABOUT THIS.

GET BACK...ALL OF YOU! WITH THE ROCKET RED'S CIRCUITRY, I COMMAND THE SHIP! YOUR COMRADES' LIVES ARE IN MY HANDS!

I DON'T GET IT... WHY'S HE ACTING THIS WAY?

WE ARE MANHUNTERS! WE HAVE PREPARED FOR EVERY CONTINGENCY!

MANHUNTERS? OH, BOY-- THAT EXPLAINS IT!

BWOOM

HEY--

I SAID --GET *BACK!*

I THINK IT'S ONLY FAIR TO WARN YOU THAT I CAN GET PRETTY *TOUGH* WHEN I GET ANGRY!

BUT I *HATE* TO GET ANGRY!

AND I WARN *YOU:* IF YOU DO NOT LEAVE, I SHALL *DETONATE* MY ARMOR! THE SHIP WILL EXPLODE! BATMAN AND THE OTHERS WILL *DIE!*

WELL, THAT *DOES* LIMIT OUR OPTIONS...

HERE'S *ANOTHER* PROBLEM, J'ONN -- WE'RE HEADING INTO BIALYAN AIRSPACE!

OPINION, BOOSTER: DO YOU THINK HE'S BLUFFING?

NO TIME TO FIGURE THAT OUT--

--LOOK!

THE SHIP'S SPEEDING RIGHT FOR THAT *OIL REFINERY!* IF IT HITS--!

WHEN IT HITS...THOUSANDS OF LIVES WILL BE LOST! THE JUSTICE LEAGUE WILL DIE... AND DIE IN *DISGRACE!*

FOR *THEY* WILL BE BLAMED FOR THIS DISASTER!

THE MANHUNTERS WILL TRIUMPH!

I'LL SAY *THIS* FOR THE MANHUNTERS--THEY REALLY SEEM TO *LIKE* THEIR JOBS.

WHERE ARE THE *OTHERS* GOING?

WHERE THEY *MUST.* CIVILIAN *LIVES* ARE AT STAKE.

AND *US?*

WE'RE *EXPENDABLE.*

OH, I *KNEW* THAT.

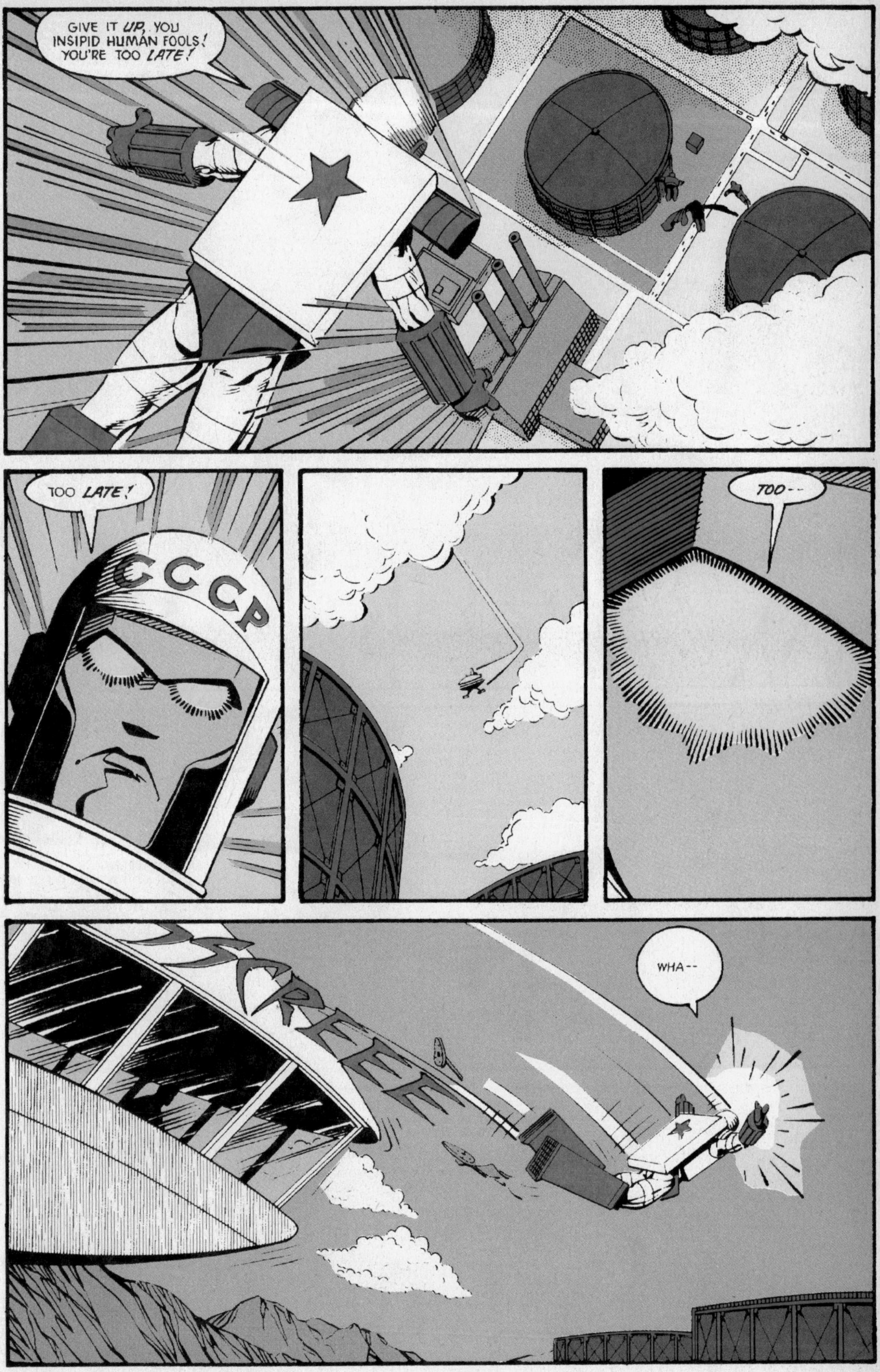
GIVE IT UP, YOU INSIPID HUMAN FOOLS! YOU'RE TOO LATE!
TOO LATE!
CCCP
TOO--
WHA--
SKREEEE

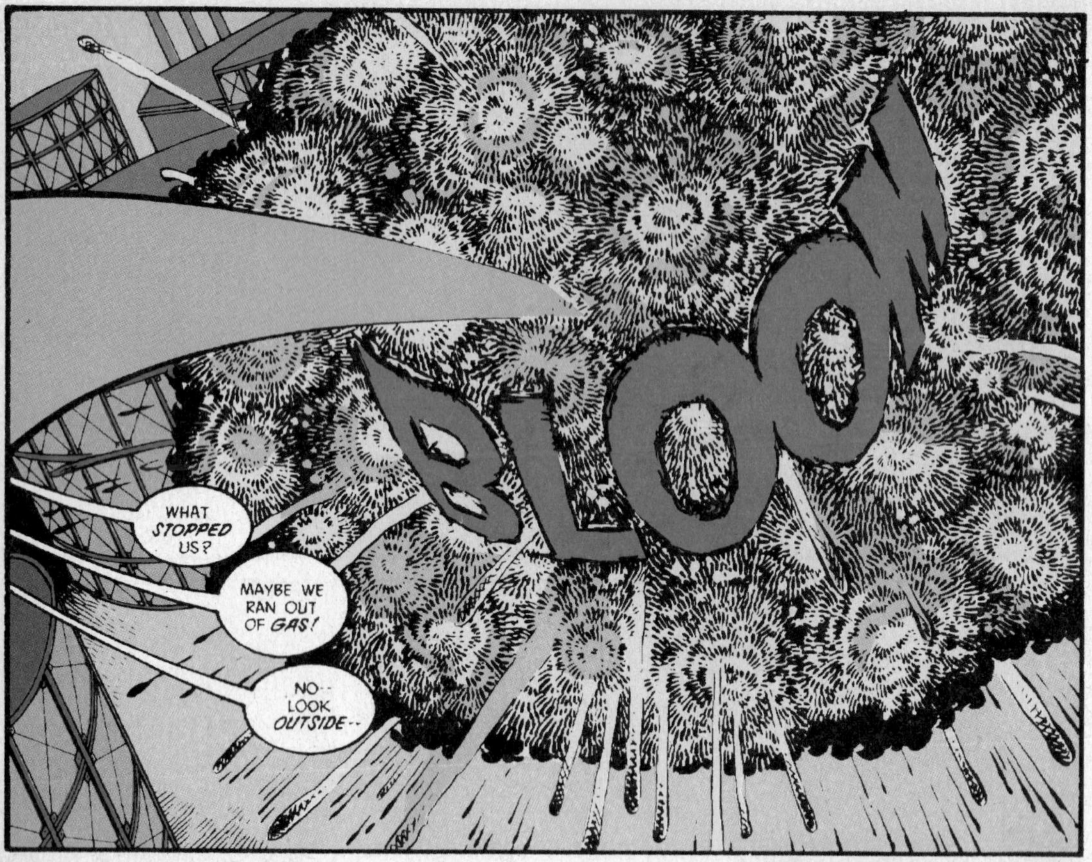
BLOOM
WHAT STOPPED US?
MAYBE WE RAN OUT OF GAS!
NO-- LOOK OUTSIDE--

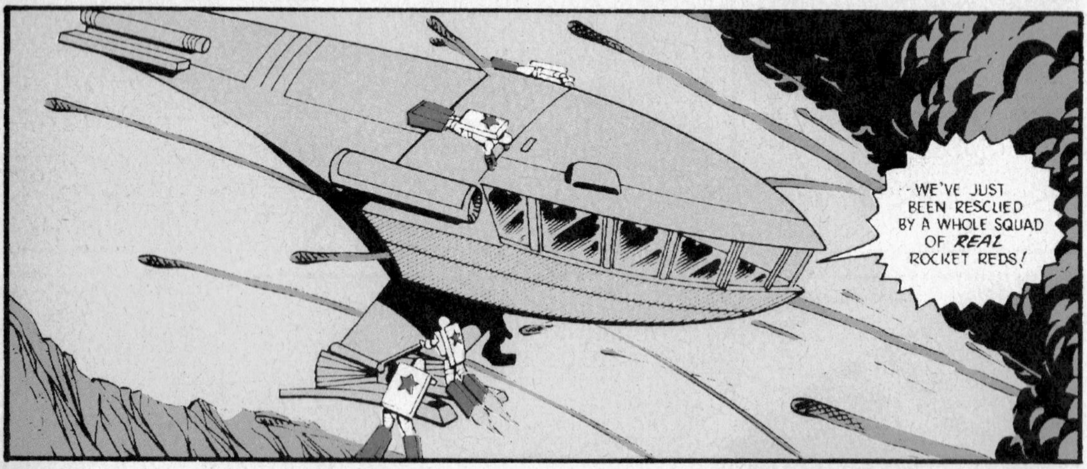
--WE'VE JUST BEEN RESCUED BY A WHOLE SQUAD OF REAL ROCKET REDS!

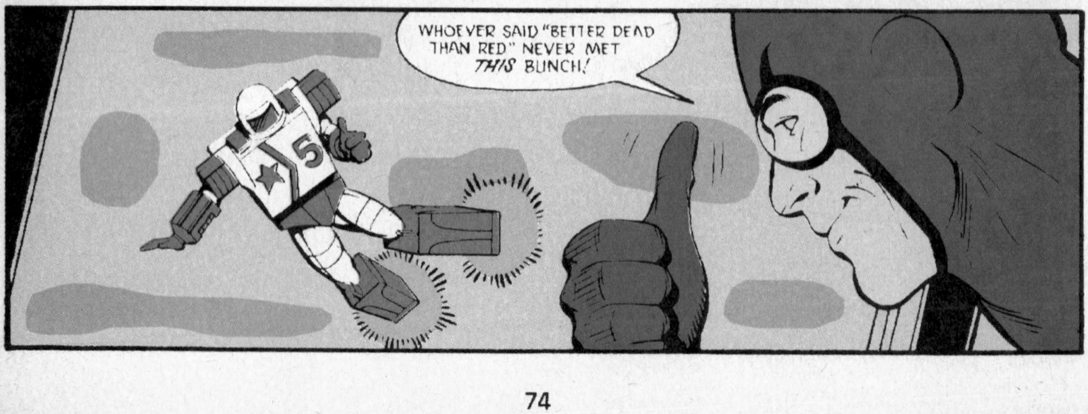
WHOEVER SAID "BETTER DEAD THAN RED" NEVER MET THIS BUNCH!
5

HI, GUYS. I...UH...GUESS I'M A LITTLE *LATE*, HUH?

THAT ALL DEPENDS: DID YOU BRING ANYTHING TO EAT?

NO.

THEN YOU'RE *LATE!*

HI, THERE, CAPTAIN ATOM-- I'LL BE DOWN IN A FLASH...JUST AS SOON AS I'M DONE CONTAINING THIS FIRE!

TAKE YOUR *TIME!*

...SO IT SEEMS OUR LITTLE BUDDY *OBERON* RADIOED OUR NEAREST ACTIVE *EMBASSY* WHEN HE SMELLED TROUBLE.

THE *SOVIET* EMBASSY.

YUP. AND QUICK AS YOU COULD SAY *GOGOL'S OVERCOAT*-- THEY CAME A'RUNNIN'!

"GOGOL'S OVERCOAT"? I DON'T UNDERSTAND.

IT'S A FAMOUS RUSSIAN STORY. *YOU* KNOW--GOGOL? "THE OVERCOAT"?

GOGOL *WHO?*

GOGOL *WHO?*

HE IS HAVING *FUN* WITH YOU, COMRADE BEETLE.

"HAVING FUN"? YOU MEAN HE WAS *JOKING?* DON'T YOU THINK THAT'S SLIGHTLY...*IMMATURE?*

...YOU HAVE OUR THANKS.

AND YOU CAN HAVE THE BLUE BEETLE, AS WELL.

VERY FUNNY!

NO, COMRADE--YOU MAY KEEP HIM, BUT *WE* WILL REPLACE OUR DISGRACED--

A-HA!

< I MIGHT HAVE *KNOWN* THAT IT WAS THE *JUSTICE LEAGUE* WHO HAS SO BRAZENLY INVADED MY NATION FOR A *SECOND* TIME! >

OH, NO...

RUMAAN HARJAVTI. TYRANT DICTATOR. RULER OF THE TERRORIST NATION OF *BIALYA*.

⟨ IF I KNEW WHAT YOU WERE SAYING, YOU CAPITALIST SCUM-- I WOULD SLAP YOUR FACE! ⟩

⟨ THEN ALLOW ME TO TRANSLATE IT INTO YOUR LANGUAGE. ⟩

⟨ NO-- DON'T BOTHER! IT WILL BE ENOUGH FOR ME TO REPORT TO MY SOVIET *ALLIES* ABOUT THIS INCURSION... THIS FLAGRANT ACT OF *WAR*... THIS-- ⟩

⟨ YOUR "SOVIET ALLIES" WERE *RESPONSIBLE* FOR THIS UNINTENTIONAL INCURSION, COLONEL HARJAVTI. ⟩

⟨ WELL, THEN... I... UH... THAT IS... ⟩

FIRE'S BURNED OUT! THE CRISIS IS *PAST!*

AND, GOSH-- ISN'T IT A *LOVELY* DAY?

THE DAY... IS NOT... QUITE *OVER* YET...

I HAVE... ONE MISSILE LEFT... ENOUGH POWER... TO DESTROY... DISCREDIT...

I HAVE... POWER TO... *WIN*.

NO MAN...ESCAPES...
THE MANHUNTERS.

BLONG

〈WHO‽〉

WHAT?

KOSMOS!?

NICE JOB, M'BOY.

I COULDN'T HAVE DONE BETTER *MYSELF.*

NO, NO--DON'T THANK *ME*--THANK MY TRUSTY *FORCE-FIELD PROJECTOR.*

ON *SECOND* THOUGHT-- THANK *ME!*

GOOD *WORK,* BOOSTER-BUDDY! THIS ALMOST MAKES UP FOR THE WAY YOU *EMBARRASSED* YOURSELF IN *PARIS* THE OTHER DAY! --*GROAN*--

〈ALL OF YOU! OUT OF MY COUNTRY! IT'S *MINE*--AND I SIMPLY WON'T *HAVE* YOU HERE!〉

〈JUST BECAUSE YOUR RIDICULOUS *UNITED NATIONS* RECOGNIZES YOU, DOES NOT MEAN THAT COLONEL RUMAAN HARJAVTI MUST!〉

A MOST... *PECULIAR* LITTLE MAN.

WE'RE GOING TO HAVE MORE *TROUBLE* FROM HIM. I CAN *FEEL* IT.

BUT THE COLONEL'S UNIMPORTANT RIGHT *NOW.*

IF THE MANHUNTERS MANAGED TO GAIN ENTRY INTO THE *LEAGUE*--

--THEN THEY CAN BE VIRTUALLY *ANYWHERE,* FROM THE LOCAL CHURCH TO THE *WHITE HOUSE*--TO--

I THINK IT BEST THAT THOSE OF YOU WITH PERSONAL LIVES *SEE* TO THEM. THE PEOPLE YOU TRUST MOST--

--MIGHT VERY WELL BE *MANHUNTERS.*

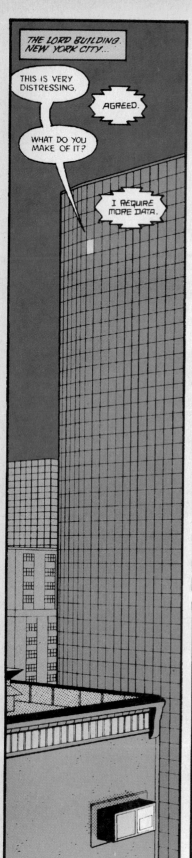

THE LORD BUILDING. NEW YORK CITY...

THIS IS VERY DISTRESSING.

AGREED.

WHAT DO YOU MAKE OF IT?

I REQUIRE MORE DATA.

I THOUGHT YOU KNEW EVERYTHING.

I AM NOT A GOD.

THAT'S NOT WHAT YOU TOLD ME.

I AM MORE DEPENDABLE...MORE EFFICIENT...THAN ANY GOD.

AND HUMBLE, TOO.

LOOK AT THIS--

--ALL OUR POTENTIAL CANDIDATES FOR LEAGUE MEMBERSHIP--

--IN SOME KIND OF PERSONAL TROUBLE BECAUSE OF THESE-- THESE--!

WHAT ARE THEY? WHO ARE THEY?

IF THEY CAN GET THIS CLOSE TO SOMEONE LIKE WONDER WOMAN--

I AM EXTENDING MY WEB. I AM ANALYZING.

WHILE *YOU'RE* ANALYZING-- ALL *HELL'S* BREAKING LOOSE!

EVEN *SUPERMAN*-- THE GREATEST, THE MOST *INVULNERABLE* OF EARTH'S HEROES-- HAS FOUND HIS LIFE *CORRUPTED* BY THEM!

AND NOW WE'VE LOST CONTACT WITH THE *LEAGUE*--

DAMMIT!

I'VE GOT TO KNOW WHAT'S GOING *ON!*

WORKING.

I WILL HAVE AN ANSWER PRESENTLY. BE PATIENT.

I'M NOT A PATIENT *MAN.*

MR. *LORD....?*

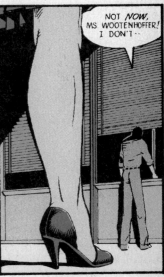

NOT *NOW,* MS WOOTENHOFFER! I DON'T··

BUT IT'S *IMPORTANT,* SIR. A MEMO.

I DON'T *CARE* ABOUT ANY DAMN

--MEMOS··

YOU'LL CARE ABOUT *THIS* ONE.

ARGGHH!

READY FOR THAT *MEMO*, MR. LORD?

POP

NO MAN ESCAPES THE MANHUNTERS.

WILL THERE BE ANYTHING *ELSE*, MISTER L--

KLIK...KLICK KLIC

WHRIRR

OH, NO

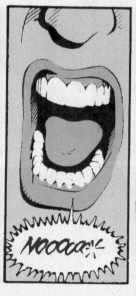

NOOOOO!

YOU'VE BEEN A VERY BAD GIRL, MS. WOOTENHOFFER.

L LORD IV

80

LATER THAT MILLENNIUM...

O.K., fasten your seatbelts, a lot happens in the four short weeks between issues. A lot of those nean 'n' masty Manhunters have been destroyed by those intrepid and bold super-hunks and hunkettes of Earth, but it has cost them dearly. While the Guardians explain the Universe to the Chosen (don't get us started), the heroes determine the time has come to start taking the offensive, and they pick a ten-hero team to assault the Manhunter home-planet to prevent any reinforcement androids from replenishing their ranks on Earth.

For completists, where Captain Atom and Firestorm go on page 2 is to the planet's sur-face. It seems hot-head sensed someone in trouble. That someone was Harbinger, one of the Chosen, and Driq, one of the members of the Green Lantern Corps. After a quick "mistak-en identity battle," they defeat the Manhunters attacking them and escape just in time. In time for what? See the end of the issue you're about to read.

Oh, that mysterious voice that was talking to Max at the end of last issue? Don't worry. We'll get to that. All in bad time.

Be back soon.

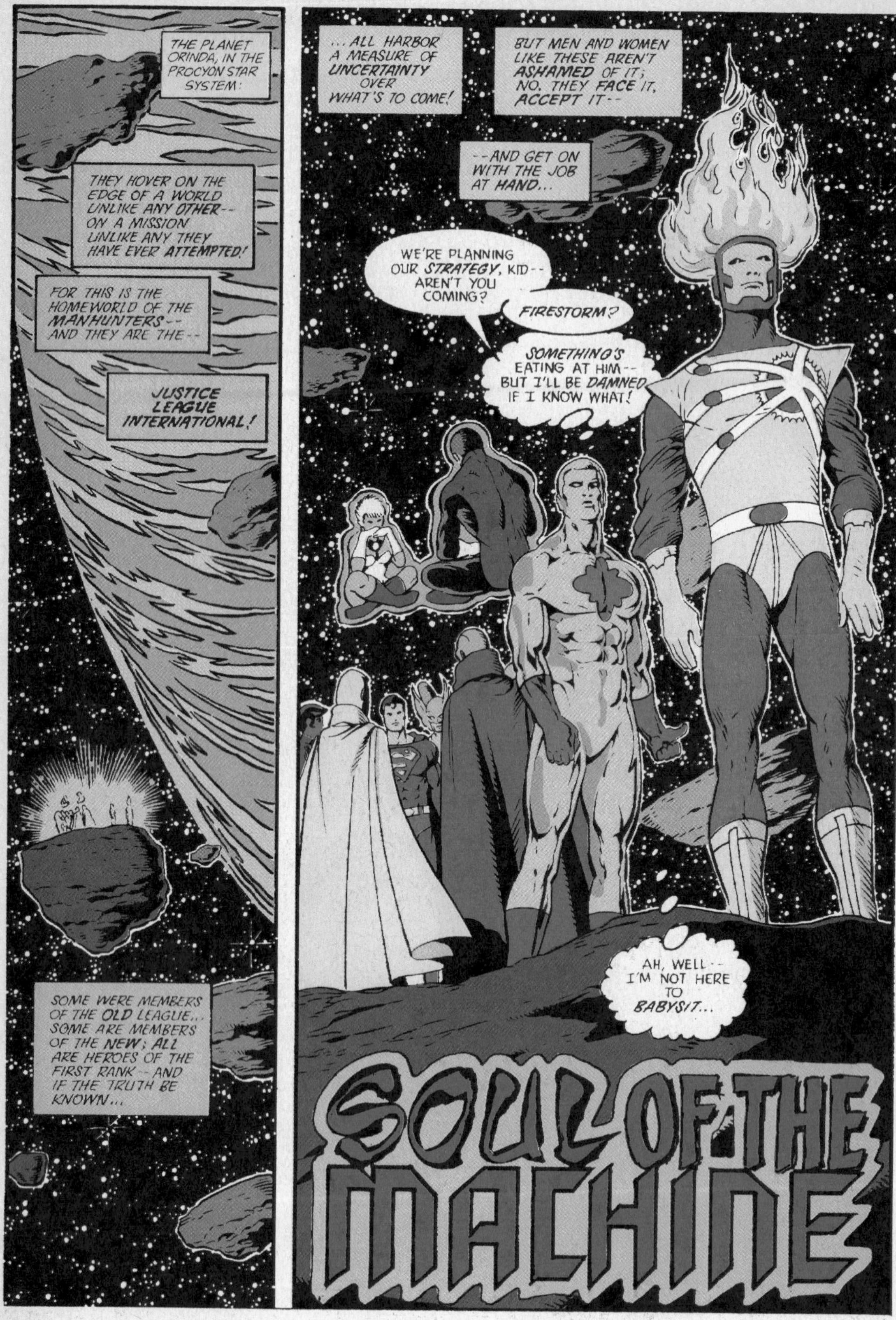
THE PLANET ORINDA, IN THE PROCYON STAR SYSTEM:
THEY HOVER ON THE EDGE OF A WORLD UNLIKE ANY OTHER-- ON A MISSION UNLIKE ANY THEY HAVE EVER ATTEMPTED!
FOR THIS IS THE HOMEWORLD OF THE MANHUNTERS-- AND THEY ARE THE--
JUSTICE LEAGUE INTERNATIONAL!
SOME WERE MEMBERS OF THE OLD LEAGUE... SOME ARE MEMBERS OF THE NEW; ALL ARE HEROES OF THE FIRST RANK-- AND IF THE TRUTH BE KNOWN...
...ALL HARBOR A MEASURE OF UNCERTAINTY OVER WHAT'S TO COME!
BUT MEN AND WOMEN LIKE THESE AREN'T ASHAMED OF IT; NO, THEY FACE IT, ACCEPT IT--
--AND GET ON WITH THE JOB AT HAND...
WE'RE PLANNING OUR STRATEGY, KID-- AREN'T YOU COMING?
FIRESTORM?
SOMETHING'S EATING AT HIM-- BUT I'LL BE DAMNED IF I KNOW WHAT!
AH, WELL-- I'M NOT HERE TO BABYSIT...
SOUL OF THE MACHINE

BUT IT COULDN'T *HURT* T'GIVE IT ONE MORE CRACK...

C'MON, KID-- WHAT'S THE *PROBLEM?*

YOU COULD AT *LEAST* GIVE ME THE COURTESY OF A REPLY! A SIMPLE "STICK IT UP YOUR--"

HEY!

NOW WHAT?

THAT'S WHAT *I'D* LIKE TO KNOW, J'ONN!

I CAN GET HIM BACK BEFORE HE--

UH-UH, *SUPERMAN*-- YOU'RE NEEDED *HERE!* I'LL HANDLE THIS! BESIDES--

--FIRESTORM SEEMS TO HAVE BECOME MY *PERSONAL* PROBLEM LATELY! YOU COULD ALMOST SAY I'VE GROWN *FOND* OF THE KID.

ALMOST.

BE CAREFUL, *CAPTAIN!*

YES, MOTHER!

SO MUCH FOR THE ELEMENT OF *SURPRISE.*

THIS IS PAR FOR THE COURSE FOR THE LEAGUE.

IT WASN'T IN THE *OLD* DAYS.

IN CASE YOU HAVEN'T NOTICED, *HAWKMAN*--THE OLD DAYS ARE LONG *GONE!*

JUST THINK-- I'VE ONLY BEEN IN THIS SUPER-HERO GAME FOR A FEW SHORT MONTHS-- AND HERE I AM, HALFWAY ACROSS THE GALAXY, CHASING A NUCLEAR-HEADED ADOLESCENT WITH AN ATTITUDE PROBLEM!

MAKES A GUY WONDER WHAT'LL HAPPEN *NEXT!**

TIME IS OF THE *ESSENCE!* WE MUST ACT NOW--BEFORE WE'RE *NOTICED!*

IF WE HAVEN'T BEEN NOTICED *ALREADY!*

I SEE NO REASON FOR YOUR *BELLIGERENCE,* HAWKMAN!

OH, J'ONN--YOU SHOULD KNOW BY NOW THAT KATAR'S NOT BEING *BELLIGERENT*--

--HE'S JUST BEING *HIMSELF!*

WELL, THEN--PERHAPS HE CAN SHARE HIS *WISDOM* WITH US. AFTER ALL, HE *IS* A MASTER OF THANAGARIAN STRATEGY--A MEMBER OF THEIR POLICE--

NOT ANYMORE. I'M NO LONGER AFFILIATED WITH THANAGAR--IN *ANY* WAY!

WHAT A TRAGEDY FOR YOUR HOMEWORLD.

WAS THAT A *DIG?*

PERISH THE THOUGHT.

HEY--*DOCTOR FATE!*

YES, *ARISIA?*

CAN'T YOU JUST WAVE YOUR MAGIC WAND AND ZAP ALL THE MANHUNTERS INTO ANOTHER *DIMENSION* OR SOMETHING?

I'M AFRAID IT'S NOT THAT *SIMPLE.*

THE ENERGY I'M EXPENDING TO BYPASS THIS PLANET'S CLOAKING DEVICE AND MAKE IT *VISIBLE* TO US IS SEVERELY LIMITING MY *CAPABILITIES.*

BUT I'D HEARD THAT YOU WERE PRACTICALLY *ALL-POWERFUL!* THAT YOU COULD--

I'M AFRAID THAT YOU HEARD *WRONG.*

BECAUSE THAT WAS *ANOTHER* DR. FATE-- AND I...*WE*...HAVE FAR TO GO BEFORE WE CAN ATTAIN *HIS* LEVEL...

OKAY, PEOPLE-- LET'S MOVE *OUT!*

WE'VE GOT US A *WAR* TO *WIN!!*

84

THAT MIGHT NOT BE SO *HARD*-- CONSIDERING WE'RE NOT MEETING ANY *RESISTANCE!*

THIS IS DAMN *PECULIAR.*

THE ENTIRE PLANET APPEARS TO BE TOTALLY *BARREN!*

LET ME JUST TAKE A LONG-RANGE SCAN WITH MY *TELESCOPIC VISION*--

HAL! ALL THE *ROCKS*--

YELLOW, I KNOW.

YOU THINK MAYBE SOMEBODY WAS *EXPECTING* A TRIO OF *GREEN LANTERNS?*

IT'S NOT JUST THE ROCKS! THERE'S A FINE YELLOW *DUST* IN THE AIR. OUR RINGS ARE *USELESS* UP HERE!

THE MANHUNTERS KNOW ABOUT THE *IMPURITY* IN YOUR RINGS! THIS *HAS* TO BE A SET-UP!

YELLOW ROCKS...YELLOW *DUST*...IT'S ALMOST AS IF IT WERE ALL MADE TO *ORDER!*

I'M AFRAID THAT'S THE *ANSWER,* J'ONN

--IT WAS!!

POOM

85

I'LL SAY *THIS* FOR YOU, SUPERMAN --

-- YOU KNOW HOW TO MAKE A *POINT!*

YOU CAN'T *FAULT* HIM FOR LACK OF *STYLE!*

HE'S A BIT TOO *THEATRICAL* FOR MY TASTE.

MISTER *ROGERS* IS TOO THEATRICAL FOR *YOUR* TASTE, DARLING...

THIS IS WHAT I GET FOR WORKING WITH MY *WIFE.*

...THE WHOLE PLANET -- IS A *MACHINE!* IT MAKES SENSE -- A MACHINE RACE *WOULD* COME FROM A MACHINE *WORLD!*

EVERYTHING'S YELLOW! IT'S A WONDER THE MANHUNTERS DIDN'T PAINT *THEMSELVES* YELLOW!

SPEAKING OF --

-- WHERE *ARE* THE MANHUNTERS?

WE SHOULDN'T BE ABLE TO JUST WALTZ *IN* HERE LIKE THIS...

IT COULD BE A *TRAP...*

IT OBVIOUSLY *IS* A TRAP, *KATMA TUI* -- BUT THE QUESTION IS -- WHAT *KIND?*

ISN'T IT *OBVIOUS?*

HEADS *UP!*

LOOKS LIKE THE TRAP'S BEING SPRUNG -- RIGHT *NOW!*

CLANK

HEY, HEY, *HEY!* WHAT'S...UH... GOIN' *ON* HERE?

SOME KINDA *CONVENTION* OR SOMETHIN'?

WHY...IT'S *ANOTHER* GREEN LANTERN!

OH, NO.

HAL-- WHAT'S *WRONG?*

OH... *NO!*

HEY...I...UH...HOPE YOU CAN EXCUSE THE WAY I LOOK--BUT...UH...JUST BETWEEN YOU AN' ME --

--IT'S LIKE A *SEWER* DOWN THERE!

HEY! YOU'RE A THANAGARIAN *COP!* COME T'CHECK UP ON ME, I'LL BET!

WELL, DON'T YOU WORRY, HAWKY-BOY-- I'VE GOT EVERYTHING UNDER *CONTROL!*

WHO *ARE* YOU?!

GNORT'S THE NAME!

GREEN LANTERN OF SECTOR 68!

OR IS THAT 69?

OR IS THAT--

WHO *IS* THIS --

IDIOT. THE WORD YOU'RE LOOKING FOR IS *IDIOT!*

HIS *UNCLE* WAS A VERY *INFLUENTIAL*--MEMBER OF THE G.L. CORPS--

--AND HE SORT OF... *PUSHED* GNORT THROUGH.

THE GUARDIANS ASSIGNED HIM THIS SECTOR BECAUSE IT'S TOTALLY DEVOID OF LIFE! AND WITH THE *CLOAKING DEVICE*-- THEY NEVER EVEN KNEW THIS PLANET EXISTED!

I SALUTE YOUR *COURAGE*, FRIEND! TAKING ON THE MANHUNTERS BY YOURSELF!

HOW LONG HAVE YOU *BEEN* HERE?

LEMME SEE...UH...MAYBE UHH...THREE MONTHS?

I WAS--UH...JUST CRUISIN' THROUGH SPACE--TILL I BUMPED INTO THIS INVISIBLE WORLD! ONCE I FOUND A WAY *IN*, I GOT KINDA *LOST* DOWN HERE!

BY THE WAY... UH...WHAT'S A *MANHUNTER?*

SUPERMAN...A MOMENT OF YOUR TIME, PLEASE...

GREEN LANTERN WOULD LIKE A WORD WITH YOU...

WE'VE GOT TO *LOSE* THIS YO-YO... FAST!

DO YOU REALLY THINK IT'S *FAIR*-- CALLING HIM A "YO-YO"?

BELIEVE ME, SUPERMAN-- I'M BEING *KIND.*

WORST PART OF IT IS-- THEY DON'T EVEN HAVE A *JOHN* IN HERE!

THANK YOU FOR SHARING THAT WITH ME.

THERE!!

I CAN *FEEL* IT-- TOUCHING MY MIND!

FEEL *WHAT?*

A CENTRAL *INTELLIGENCE!* AN EXTRAORDINARY *POWER!*

OH, THAT.

WHAT DID YOU JUST SAY, FATE?

GNORT. THE NAME IS *GNO*--

I WASN'T TALKING TO *YOU*...

THERE'S A VAST *POWER SOURCE* WITHIN THIS WORLD. I ASSUME THAT'S WHERE THE MANHUNTERS ARE--

--*PROTECTING* IT!

WHERE?

DON'T *LOOK* AT ME!

BEYOND THE NEXT CORNER--

--BUT I *WARN* YOU...I COULD FEEL THE INTELLIGENCE *PROBING* US! THEY KNOW WE'RE *COMING!*

LET'S *GO!*

GNORT-- YOU STAY HERE AND GUARD THE... UH... *JOHN!*

AND WHATEVER YOU DO--DON'T LET ANY *MANHUNTERS* IN!

HEY! I...UH...TOLD YOU I NEVER DID *FIND* IT!

THEN START *LOOKING,* GNORT! THE REPUTATION OF THE ENTIRE CORPS *DEPENDS* ON IT!

THEY'RE COMING?

THEY'RE COMING.

STRAIGHT FOR US?

STRAIGHT FOR US.

EXCELLENT.

WE LOOK *FORWARD* TO THE *SLAUGHTER*.

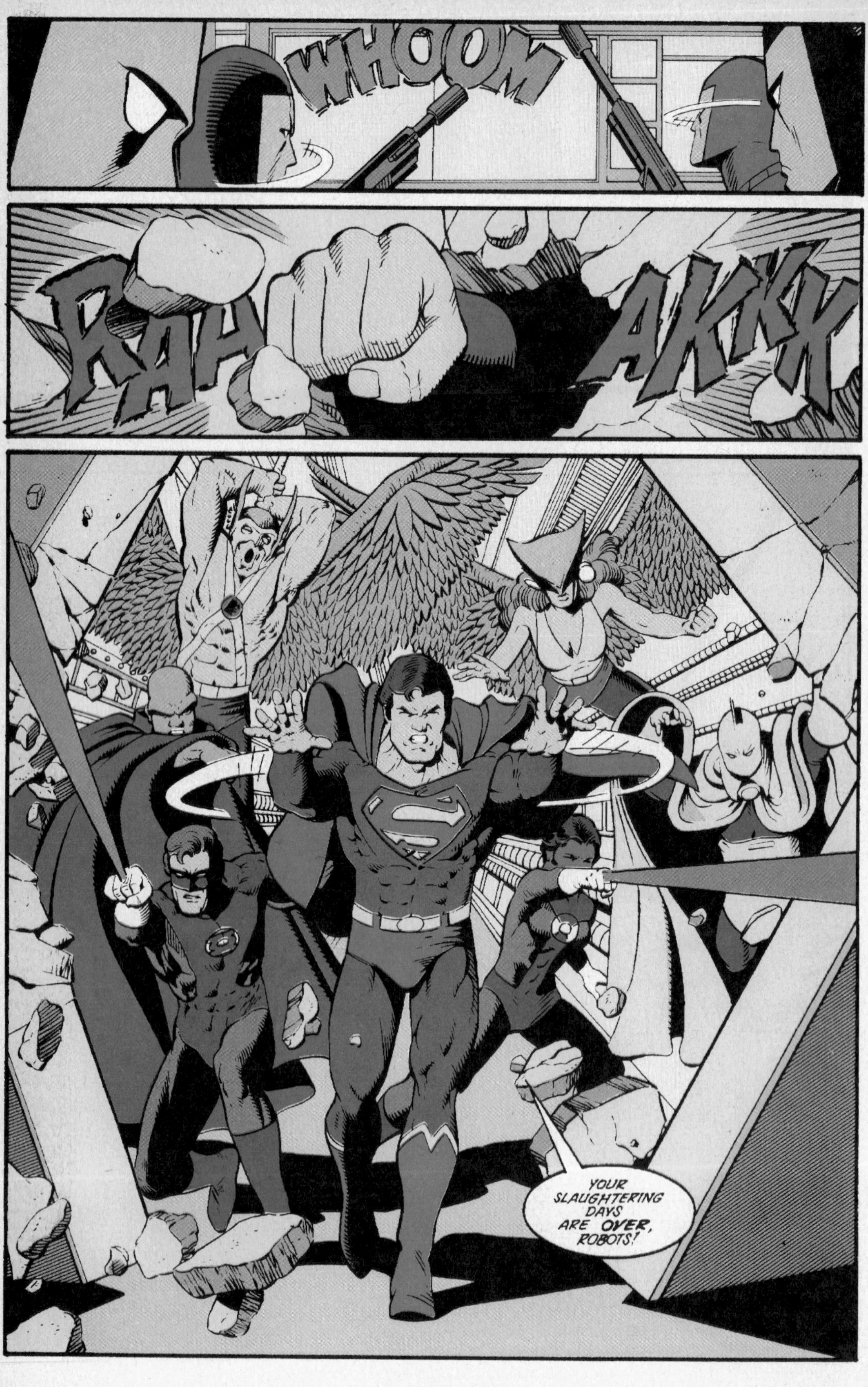
WHOOM
RAAKKK
YOUR SLAUGHTERING DAYS ARE OVER, ROBOTS!

IMPOSSIBLE! OUR SENSORS STILL SHOW THEM IN CORRIDOR 75!

THAT'S *MILES* FROM HERE!

FRIM! DON'T KNOW WHY J'ONN MADE *ME* CREATE THESE DECOYS AND DRAG THEM THROUGH THESE DARN HALLWAYS! BUT WHATEVER HIS REASONS--

I JUST HOPE THEY *WORK!*

IT DOES.

THE MANHUNTERS WERE ANTICIPATING A SLAUGHTER. THAT'S EXACTLY WHAT THEY GET.

BECAUSE IN LESS THAN SIXTY SECONDS, THE WORLD'S *GREATEST* SUPER-HEROES...

...LIVE UP TO THEIR NAME!

BY THE DOZENS...

...BY THE HUNDREDS...

...THE MANHUNTERS...

...FALL!

...THE EMANATIONS GROW STRONGER IN THIS DIRECTION.

BUT WE'VE GOT TO *PINPOINT* THEM EXACTLY!

NOW WHAT WAS IT KENT TOLD US? RAISE THE ENERGY UP THE *CHAKRAS*-- FOCUS THE THIRD EYE AND --

--THERE!

IT'S *OVER.*

THUK

I *ENJOYED* THAT!

I HATE TO ADMIT IT, BUT SO DID *I!*

REMINDED ME OF THE WAY IT *USED* TO BE.

RIGHT-- WHEN THE JUSTICE LEAGUE WAS TRUSTWORTHY... *DEPENDABLE*--

DULL... THICK-HEADED...

J'ONN, I COULD NOT HELP BUT NOTICE THAT YOU ARE NOT AS... *STOIC* AS I HAD IMAGINED YOU TO BE...

WHY, KATMA-- WHATEVER DO YOU *MEAN?*

OH, HAL HAS TOLD US MANY STORIES OF YOUR--

HEY-- DID ANYONE SEE WHERE DOCTOR FATE WENT?

HE WENT *THATAWAY!*

YOU KNOW-- I'VE BEEN WAITING *YEARS* TO SAY THAT!

SHAYERA--HOW CAN YOU *JOKE* AT A TIME LIKE THIS?

GUESS IT'S *SECOND NATURE* BY NOW...

I THINK EXHIBITING A SENSE OF HUMOR IN THE FACE OF DANGER IS *ADMIRABLE*, HAWKWOMAN.

WHY, *THANK* YOU, SUPERMAN.

"WHY, THANK YOU, SUPERMAN!"

HANG *ON* A SEC-- I DON'T WANT TO GO *ANYWHERE* UNTIL WE'VE FOUND--

ME?

ARISIA! HONEY--I WAS *WORRIED* ABOUT YOU!

WELL, WORRY NO MORE! HERE I AM--BIG AS LIFE AND TWICE AS CUTE!

DID I *MISS* ANYTHING?

JUST THE *APPETIZER*--I'VE A HUNCH YOU'RE *IN TIME* FOR THE *MAIN COURSE*--

WHAT *IS* THIS PLACE, DOCTOR--?

INCREDIBLE. THE GUARDIANS TOLD US OF THE SEEMINGLY IMMORTAL ANDROIDS--BUT THEY NEVER *SUGGESTED* THEIR THREAT WAS AN ONGOING CONCERN!

THIS *PLACE*--IT *PERPETUATES* THE MANHUNTERS' EVIL--I CAN FEEL THE POTENTIALLY *LIMITLESS* ENERGY COURSING UNDER OUR FEET...FEEDING...NURTURING... WE MUST ACT TO DESTROY IT *NOW*--BEFORE--

WAIT A SEC, DOCTOR--WE STILL DON'T KNOW WHAT THIS ROOM IS SUPPOSED TO--

GREAT SCOTT! IT--IT'S A *BIRTHING CHAMBER*--!

--BUT THAT HUGE *STATUE* UP THERE-- LIKE SOME KIND OF *OVERSEER*, OR--

OVERSEER, NOTHING, SUPERMAN-- THAT'S THE BIGGEST DADDY MANHUNTER I'VE EVER SEEN!

HMM...PERHAPS *MOTHER* IS A MORE APT TERM IN THIS SITUATION, ARISIA.

AND WHILE I AGREE THAT IT IS NOT A STATUE OR EFFIGY, NEITHER DOES IT SEEM TO BE *FUNCTIONING.*

MAYBE IT'S *DISTRACTED.*

WHAT DO YOU *MEAN*--?

SHE MEANS THAT "MOTHER" JUST MIGHT BE "*GIVING BIRTH*" AS WE SPEAK!

YES, OUR PRESENCE HAS BEEN DETECTED. THEY'RE COMING TO LIFE, A BIT *PREMATURELY.*

YOUR *HEAT VISION* CAN HANDLE THIS--?

YOU MEAN, JUST *INCINERATE* THEM?

THEY'RE THE SAME AS THOSE ROBOTS WE LEFT BACK *THERE,* SUPERMAN. THEY MAY *MIMIC* LIFE--

--BUT THEY'RE *NOT ALIVE!*

QUICKLY, NOW-- WHILE THERE'S STILL *TIME!*

FZAKKKT

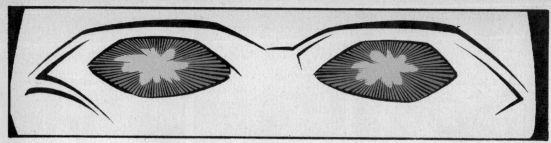

I AM THE *HIGHMASTER* OF THE MANHUNTERS--

--AND I AM *GREATLY* DISPLEASED.

YOU HAVE *SULLIED* MY HOME... *KILLED* MY CHILDREN.

WHO WERE TRYING THEIR BEST TO KILL *US!*

SILENCE!

WHO GAVE YOU PERMISSION TO *SPEAK* IN MY PRESENCE?

POP
POP
POP
POP

NO MATTER YOUR WORLD OF ORIGIN--

--YOU *FLESHLINGS* ARE BENEATH *CONTEMPT!*

IF IT'S A *FIGHT* YOU'RE LOOKING FOR--!

HARDLY.

I'M LEAVING.

I'VE CREATED ONE WORLD... IN TIME, I CAN CREATE *ANOTHER.*

WHEN MY CHILDREN ON EARTH HAVE ACCOMPLISHED THEIR GOAL, THERE WILL BE *MUCH* TIME FOR RECONSTRUCTION.

AS FOR *YOU*-- MY POWER *ALONE* HOLDS THIS PLANET TOGETHER --

--*WITHOUT* ME-- IT ALL FLIES *APART!*

SSSSS

YOU'LL *NEVER* FIND YOUR WAY TO THE SURFACE IN TIME!

RUMMMMN

UH-OH.

96

NOTHING TO WORRY ABOUT, FOLKS--

--JUST FOLLOW ME!

AMAZING.

HEY-- WHAT ABOUT GNORT?

THAT'S RIGHT! MAYBE I SHOULD GO BACK AND--

IT'S NOT LIKE THE PLANET'S BLOWING UP, SUPERMAN--IT'S JUST...FALLING APART.

GNORT'S POWER RING SHOULD KEEP HIM OUT OF HARM'S WAY.

STILL, A QUICK SCAN OF THE PLANET COULDN'T HURT--

ODD, I DON'T SEE HIM ANYWHERE!

SEE? HE'S FREE AND CLEAR ALREADY.

I JUST HOPE HE DOESN'T FOLLOW US!

GNORT MAY BE SAFE--

BUT WHAT ABOUT FIRESTORM AND CAPTAIN ATOM?

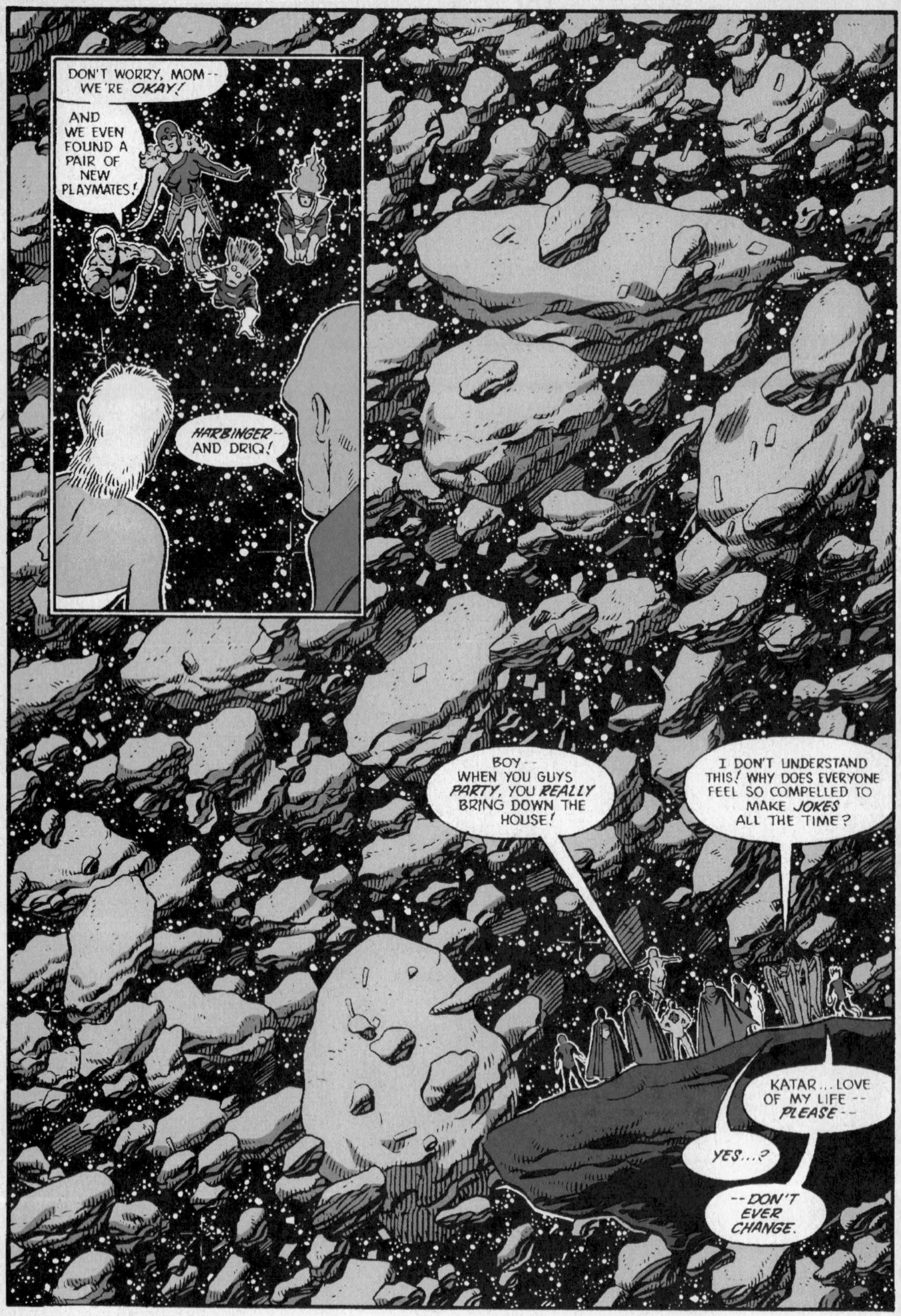
DON'T WORRY, MOM-- WE'RE OKAY!
AND WE EVEN FOUND A PAIR OF NEW PLAYMATES!
HARBINGER-- AND DRIQ!
BOY-- WHEN YOU GUYS PARTY, YOU REALLY BRING DOWN THE HOUSE!
I DON'T UNDERSTAND THIS! WHY DOES EVERYONE FEEL SO COMPELLED TO MAKE JOKES ALL THE TIME?
KATAR... LOVE OF MY LIFE-- PLEASE--
YES...?
--DON'T EVER CHANGE.

AFTER THE MILLENNIUM
(or It Ain't Over Till We Say So)

To conclude. About one second after the last splash page, the Highmaster showed up again. It seems you can't keep a good monstrous android down...or a bad one. He is defeated by Superman and Green Lantern (Hal Jordan), but there still remains all the Manhunters on Earth, which the heroes return to. Of course, our dynamic and fearless leotard-wearing protagonists defeat the manifold antagonists, the Chosen became the super-hero group called The New Guardians, and as Nadia Safir put it, "That is all there is to it." Well, at least with respect to the Millennium storyline.

Now you're on your own. The last two stories pretty much stand on their own and get down to the nitty gritty of "The Secret Gospel" mentioned in the title of this collection. So all that's left to say is...enjoy yourselves.

**—Kevin Dooley
Editor**

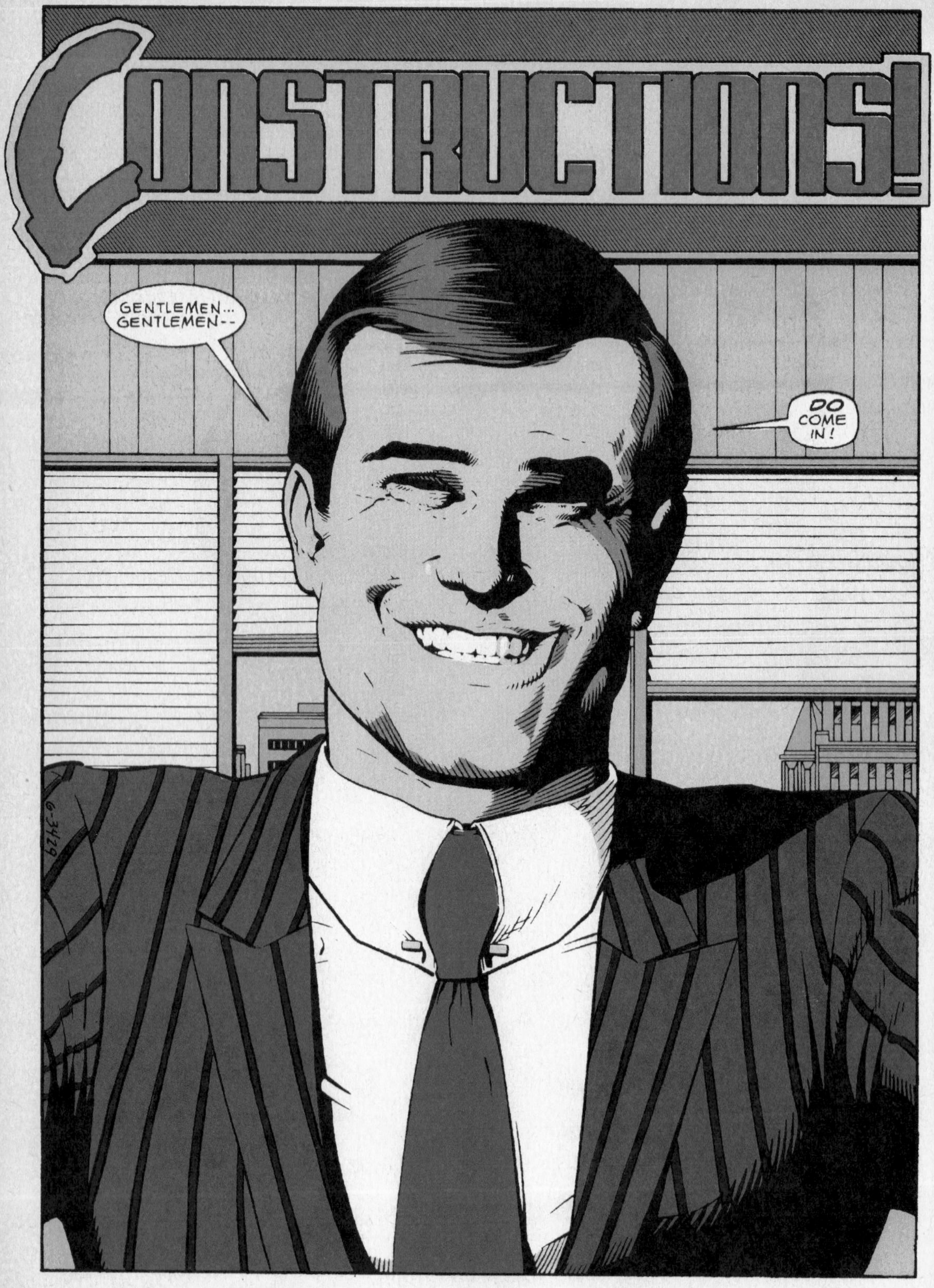
CONSTRUCTIONS!
GENTLEMEN... GENTLEMEN--
DO COME IN!

MAXWELL LORD IS ALWAYS HAPPY TO SEE HIS FAVORITE JUSTICE LEAGUERS--

--ESPECIALLY WHEN THEY'VE JUST COME BACK FROM SAVING THE UNIVERSE!*

WHAT A CONCEPT! SAVING THE *ENTIRE* UNIVERSE! ALL LIFE-FORMS ON *EVERY* PLANET SPARED A HORRIBLE DOOM BECAUSE MY *J.L. I*--

*LAST ISSUE, OF COURSE --ANDY

MAX?

YES, J'ONN?

ENOUGH?

ENOUGH.

ENOUGH.

I WAS KIND OF *ENJOYING* IT.

YOU SUMMONED US HERE TO YOUR OFFICE. *WHY?*

I'D PREFER TO WAIT FOR THE OTHERS BEFORE I BEGIN EXPLAINING.

WHAT OTHERS?

THE OTHER *HEROES* YOU WENT TO THE *MANHUNTER WORLD* WITH... *SUPERMAN, HAWKMAN,* THE *ORIGINAL GREEN LANTERN*--

THAT GROUP WAS *TEMPORARY,* MAX.

WE GATHERED TOGETHER TO MEET THE CRISIS, AND ONCE THE CRISIS *PASSED--*

THEY'RE *GONE?*

LIKE THE *WIND.*

...*GONE...?*

HOW CAN YOU DO THIS TO ME?!?!

HOW CAN YOU STAB ME IN THE BACK LIKE THIS?!?!

HEY-- A *MINUTE* AGO WE WERE THE GREATEST THING SINCE *SLICED BREAD!*

IT'S THE HUMAN MIND AT WORK, CAPTAIN. TOTALLY *UNPREDICTABLE.*

MAX--IF YOU'D *CALM DOWN* AND *EXPLAIN...*

EXPLAIN?! AN *IDIOT* COULD SEE IT WITHOUT EXPLANATIONS!

THEN ASSUME I'M AN *IDIOT*, MAX.

I...NEED... *POWER!!*

THE *RAW POWER* SUPERMAN AND THE OTHERS COULD HAVE *PROVIDED!*

I NEED *PRIME HEROES--* NOT A BUNCH OF WEAK-KNEED *SECOND-STRINGERS!*

BOY--DID YOU HEAR WHAT HE JUST CALLED *YOU?*

PERHAPS HE WAS REFERRING TO *YOU.*

MUST'VE BEEN TALK-ING ABOUT...

...*BLUE BEETLE.*

MAYBE WE SHOULD JUST GO AND LET MAX HAVE HIS LITTLE TANTRUM *ALONE...*

AN *EXCELLENT* IDEA...

NO!! WAIT! I--

I'M SORRY.

IT'S JUST THAT--

OH, *DAMN...*

FROM THE *BEGINNING,* MAX.

I... I *NEED* THOSE HEROES... THE *BEST*... THE *GREATEST*... TO *SAVE* ME...

FROM *WHAT?*

I HAVE *ENEMIES.* YOU'RE... YOU'RE MY *LAST* HOPE...

EXPLAIN...

102

WHO'S AFTER YOU?

I'M IN TROUBLE. HE...IT'S...AFTER ME!

YOU WON'T BELIEVE ME!

TELL US!

IT'S A--AT LEAST, I THINK IT'S--A SUPER-VILLAIN!

AFTER YOU?

I KNEW YOU WOULDN'T BELIEVE ME!

I DIDN'T SAY I DIDN'T BELIEVE YOU...NOW CALM DOWN, MAX--

PLEASE-- YOU'VE GOT TO HELP ME!

GOOD. DESPITE THE LOSS OF SUPERMAN AND THE OTHERS, ALL PROCEEDS ACCORDINGLY.

NEW YORK, NEW YORK...

WELL, ROCKET RED, WHAT DO YOU THINK?

IS NICE.

SHABBY-- BUT NICE.

"SHABBY"?

I'M JUST HAVING...HOW WOULD YOU SAY?...A LITTLE FUN WITH YOU.

OH.

YOU KNOW, YOU ARE MUCH NICER AS AN ALLY, BLACK CANARY.

WHAT DO YOU--?

WHEN WE MET IN RUSSIA, YOU PUT YOUR FOOT IN MY FACE...

...IN MY MOUTH, TO BE PRECISE*--

--ALTHOUGH MY WIFE SAYS THE GAP IS...CHARMING.

* WHEN THE LEAGUE AND THE ROCKET REDS CLASHED IN ISSUE 3. --ANDY

UHHH...RIGHT.

WOULD YOU LIKE TO SEE THE REC ROOM?

YOU HAVE A ROOM JUST TO WRECK?

NO, NO-- OUR RECREATION ROOM.

I KNOW, I KNOW. I'M JUST HAVING--

"--A LITTLE FUN."

OH...BROTHER!

HOLD UP, YOU TWO -- WE'VE GOT AN A-1 *ALERT* COMIN' IN!

WHEN? FROM *WHO*? FROM *WHERE*?

WHICH QUESTION WOULD YOU LIKE ME TO ANSWER *FIRST*?

DON'T BE A WISE GUY.

HEY! I'M JUST HAVING A LITTLE *FUN* WITH YOU. -*SNICKER*-

OBERON!

OKAY!

WHEN: RIGHT NOW. FROM WHO: CAPTAIN ATOM AND THE MANHUNTER. WHERE: *MAXWELL LORD'S* OFFICE BUILDING!

ALERT THE OTHERS!

I AL-READY *DID!*

RED-- LET'S *GO!*

PLEASE, CALL ME *DMITRI*. AND *YOUR* NAME IS...?

LET'S KEEP IT BLACK CANARY, *SHALL* WE? I'M SURE YOUR WIFE WILL BE *HAPPIER* THAT WAY.

DON'T TELL ME, NOW *YOU'RE* HAVING FUN WITH *ME!*

MOVE!!

SOON, ABOARD THE *J.L.I.* SHUTTLE...

NOW BE CAREFUL, *MR. MIRACLE--S.T.A.R. LABS* SAYS THIS IS THE *ONLY* SHUTTLE THEY'VE GOT LEFT.

HEY-- IT WASN'T MY FAULT THAT I ALMOST GOT TRASHED, *BEETLE!*

WEREN'T YOU THE GUY WHO FLEW IT *THROUGH THE ROOF?*

BEETLE--ALL SUPER-TEAMS LAND THEIR SHIPS ON THE ROOF!

MIRACLE, OL' BUDDY --YOU'VE BEEN READING TOO MANY *COMIC BOOKS!*

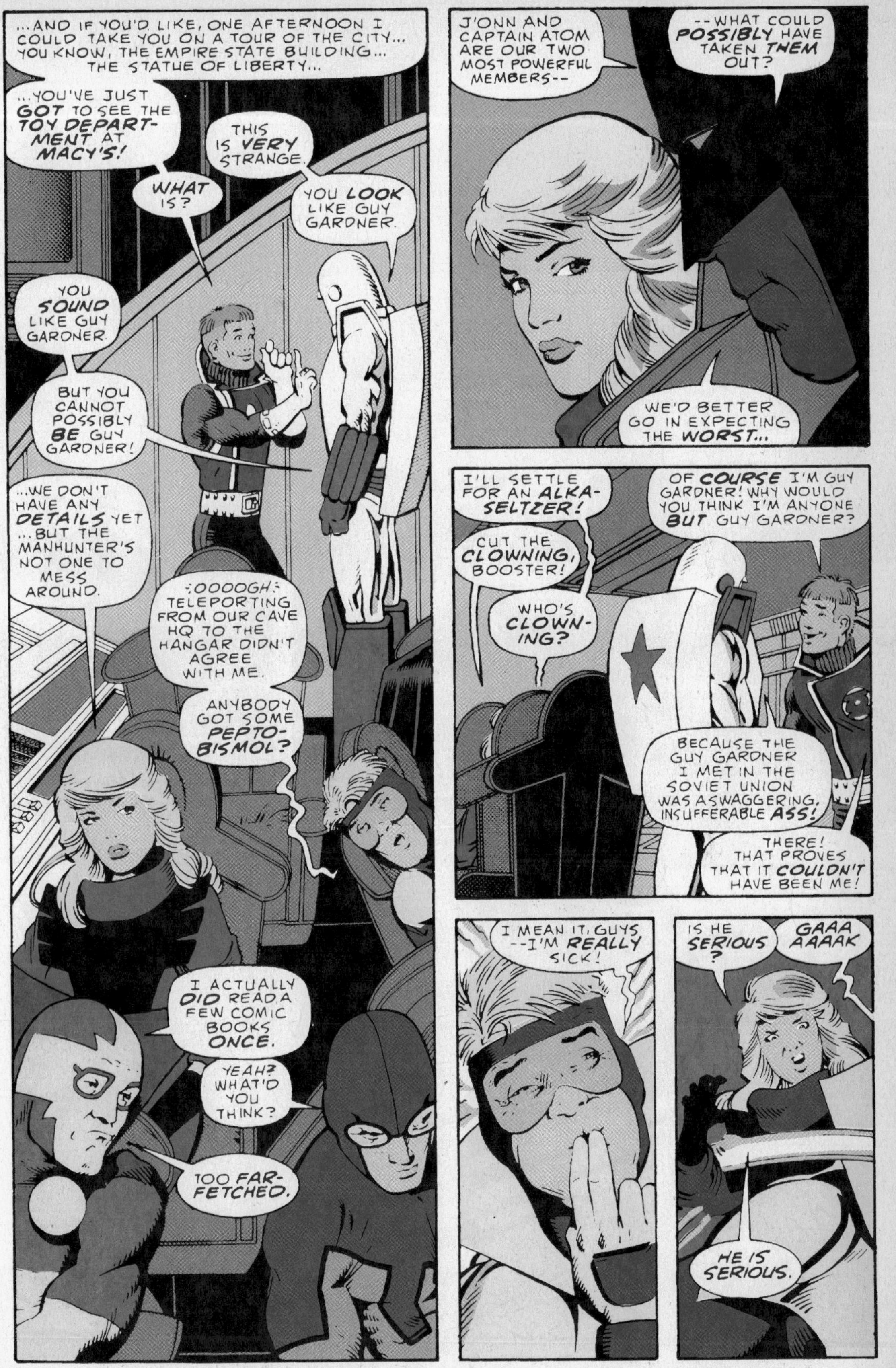
...AND IF YOU'D LIKE, ONE AFTERNOON I COULD TAKE YOU ON A TOUR OF THE CITY... YOU KNOW, THE EMPIRE STATE BUILDING... THE STATUE OF LIBERTY...
...YOU'VE JUST GOT TO SEE THE TOY DEPARTMENT AT MACY'S!
THIS IS VERY STRANGE.
WHAT IS?
YOU LOOK LIKE GUY GARDNER.
YOU SOUND LIKE GUY GARDNER.
BUT YOU CANNOT POSSIBLY BE GUY GARDNER!
...WE DON'T HAVE ANY DETAILS YET ...BUT THE MANHUNTER'S NOT ONE TO MESS AROUND.
OOOOGH TELEPORTING FROM OUR CAVE HQ TO THE HANGAR DIDN'T AGREE WITH ME.
ANYBODY GOT SOME PEPTO-BISMOL?
I ACTUALLY DID READ A FEW COMIC BOOKS ONCE.
YEAH? WHAT'D YOU THINK?
TOO FAR-FETCHED.
J'ONN AND CAPTAIN ATOM ARE OUR TWO MOST POWERFUL MEMBERS--
--WHAT COULD POSSIBLY HAVE TAKEN THEM OUT?
WE'D BETTER GO IN EXPECTING THE WORST...
I'LL SETTLE FOR AN ALKA-SELTZER!
OF COURSE I'M GUY GARDNER! WHY WOULD YOU THINK I'M ANYONE BUT GUY GARDNER?
CUT THE CLOWNING, BOOSTER!
WHO'S CLOWNING?
BECAUSE THE GUY GARDNER I MET IN THE SOVIET UNION WAS A SWAGGERING, INSUFFERABLE ASS!
THERE! THAT PROVES THAT IT COULDN'T HAVE BEEN ME!
I MEAN IT, GUYS --I'M REALLY SICK!
IS HE SERIOUS?
GAAA AAAAK
HE IS SERIOUS.

THAR SHE BLOWS!

HEY, I'M IN THE MIDDLE OF RE-READING MOBY DICK!

CALL ME BLUE ISHMAEL!

"THAR SHE BLOWS"?

I'LL BE CALLING YOU A LOT WORSE IF YOU DON'T KEEP YOUR EYES ON THE CONTROLS!

SORRY, BATS.

AND BOOSTER-- CLEAN THAT MESS UP!

HANG ON A SEC! I'M PICKING SOMETHING UP!

I DIDN'T KNOW YOU'D DROPPED ANYTHING!

SOME KIND OF ENERGY-SURGE FROM THE BUILDING. AND NOW THE RADAR'S--

DEMONS OF APOKOLIPS!

FUNNY, THEY LOOK LIKE MISSILES T'ME.

MISSILES?!

HANG ON, PEOPLE!

FWOOOOSH!

HEAT-SEEKERS! THEY'RE COMING AROUND FOR ANOTHER RUN!

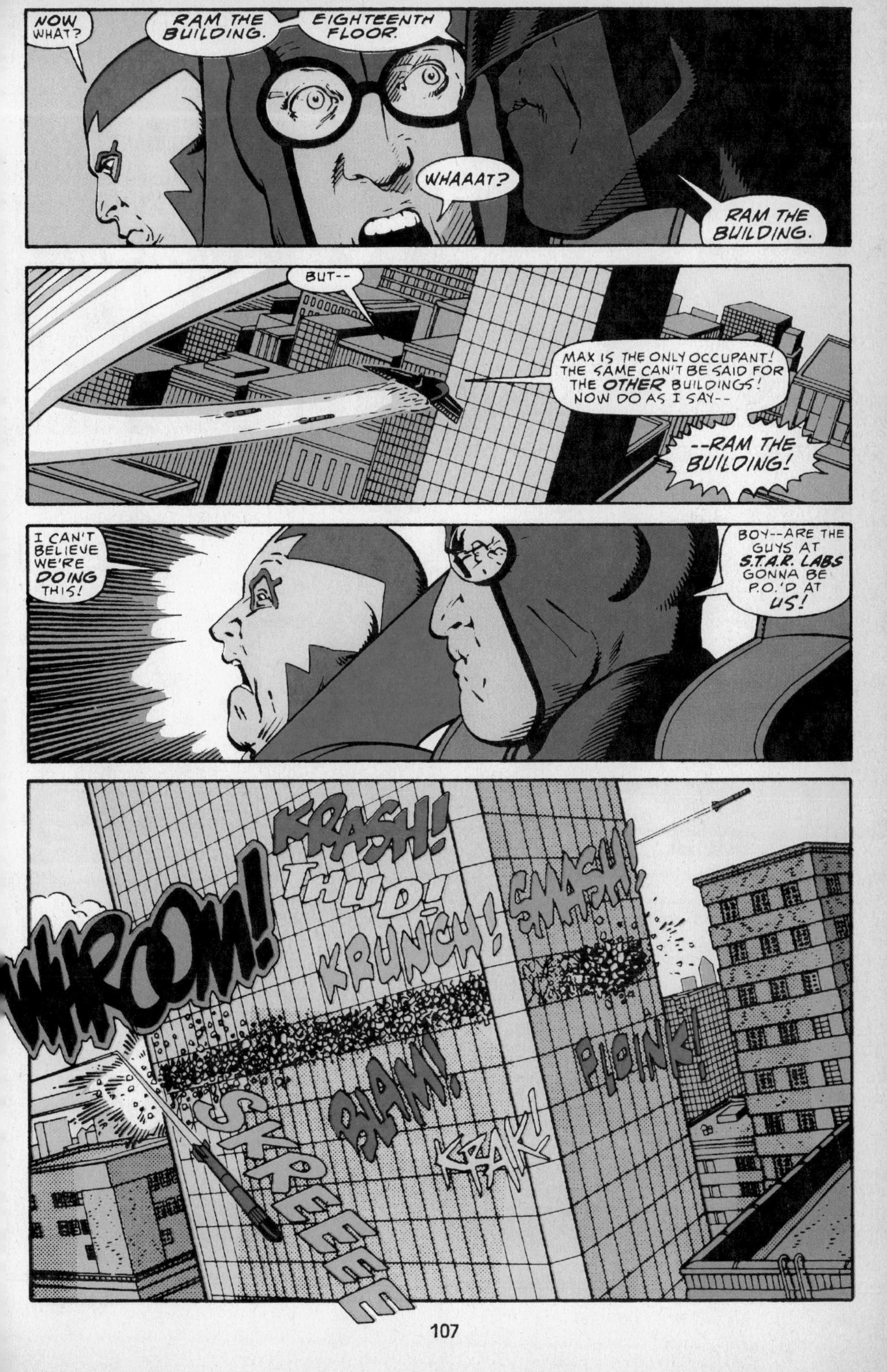
NOW WHAT?
RAM THE BUILDING.
EIGHTEENTH FLOOR.
WHAAAT?
RAM THE BUILDING.
BUT--
MAX IS THE ONLY OCCUPANT! THE SAME CAN'T BE SAID FOR THE OTHER BUILDINGS! NOW DO AS I SAY--
--RAM THE BUILDING!
I CAN'T BELIEVE WE'RE DOING THIS!
BOY--ARE THE GUYS AT S.T.A.R. LABS GONNA BE P.O.'D AT US!
WHROOM!
KRASH!
THUD!
KRUNCH!
SMASH!
PLINK!
BLAM!
SKREEEE
KRAK!

WELL, YOU'RE RIGHT. THERE *ARE* NO PEOPLE ON THIS FLOOR. HOW'D YOU *KNOW?*

I DO MY *HOMEWORK.*

BUT WHAT IF MAX HAD BEEN--

J'ONN AND CAPTAIN ATOM COULD'VE HANDLED IT.

BUT THERE *COULD'VE* BEEN INNOCENT BYSTANDERS--

THERE *WEREN'T,* WERE THERE?

MAYBE WE SHOULD CHECK THE RUBBLE TO BE *SURE.*

YOU KNOW ...I'M HAVING *FUN!*

SO *NOW* WHAT?

YOU PICKED UP THE ALERT... AND, IN THE ABSENCE OF THE TEAM LEADER, THAT PUTS *YOU* IN COM-MAND.

IT *DOES,* DOESN'T IT?

HEY--THE FLOOR! IT'S *MOVING!*

YOU'RE NOT GOING TO *THROW UP* AGAIN, ARE YOU?

RRUMMMMBLLE

LOOK! IT'S CAPTAIN ATOM--GRAPPLING WITH DOZENS OF MECHANICAL ARMS AND TENTACLES!

DID I JUST *SAY* THAT?

108

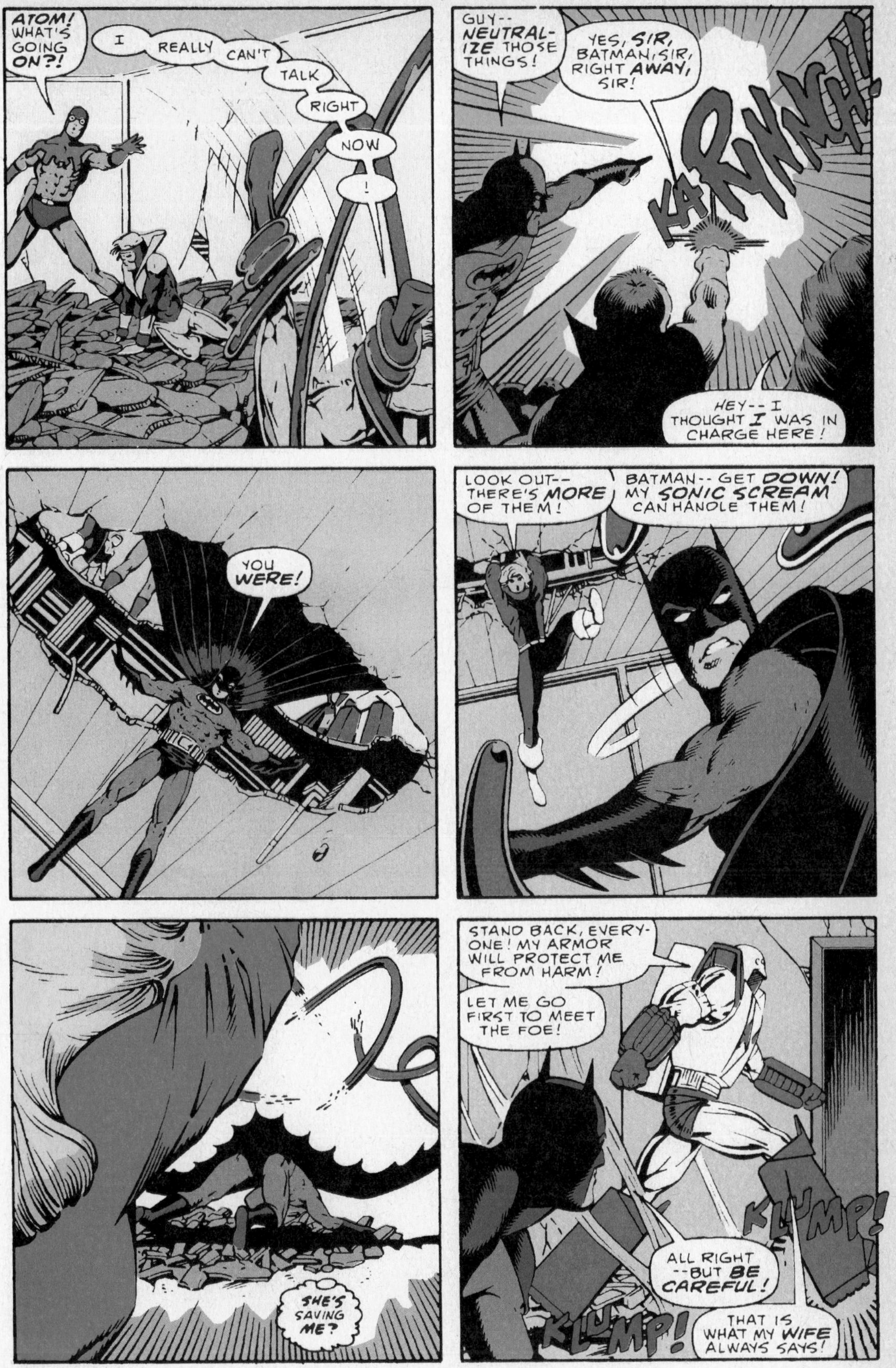
ATOM! WHAT'S GOING ON?!
I REALLY CAN'T TALK RIGHT NOW !
GUY-- NEUTRAL-IZE THOSE THINGS!
YES, SIR, BATMAN, SIR, RIGHT AWAY, SIR!
KARUNNCH!
HEY-- I THOUGHT I WAS IN CHARGE HERE!
YOU WERE!
LOOK OUT-- THERE'S MORE OF THEM!
BATMAN-- GET DOWN! MY SONIC SCREAM CAN HANDLE THEM!
SHE'S SAVING ME?
STAND BACK, EVERY-ONE! MY ARMOR WILL PROTECT ME FROM HARM!
LET ME GO FIRST TO MEET THE FOE!
KLUMP!
ALL RIGHT --BUT BE CAREFUL!
KLUMP!
THAT IS WHAT MY WIFE ALWAYS SAYS!

GOOD GRIEF! THE CORRIDORS ARE *CRAWLING* WITH THEM!

"GOOD GRIEF"?

THERE IS SOMETHING *WRONG* WITH "GOOD GRIEF"?

IT JUST DOESN'T SOUND *RIGHT* COMING FROM YOU.

I AM TRYING TO...HOW DO YOU SAY?...*PEPPER* MY LINGO WITH *AMERICANISMS.*

OH.

CANARY--THIS IS STRANGE... I'M NOT PICKING UP ANY OUTSIDE *POWER SOURCE!*

THEN THAT MUST MEAN--

I *KNOW! I KNOW!* THERE'S AN *INSIDE* POWER SOURCE!

THOSE THINGS ARE BEING CONTROLLED *IN THE BUILDING?*

BY THE BUILDING'S *ELEC-TRICITY!*

I THINK PERHAPS I AM GOING TO NEED SOME *HELP...*

HANG *IN* THERE, RED.

AS YOU WISH, *BLACK!*

OH, OKAY, *DMITRI*...YOU CAN CALL ME *DINAH!*

GUY... OVER *HERE!*

ME?

YOU!

I NEED A STRONG POWER SURGE.

HOW STRONG?

VERY STRONG!

CAN YOUR *RING*--?

I *THINK* SO. BUT I'D HATE TO LET THE TEAM *DOWN...*

THEN *DON'T*--!

OKAY.

FWASSSH!

THEY HAVE ALL BEEN DEACTIVATED!

THE WHOLE BUILDING'S BEEN DEACTIVATED!

I HOPE YOU DON'T MIND THE FACT THAT I SAVED US ALL WITHOUT CONSULTING YOU, BATMAN.

CANARY-- YOU KNOW I'M ABOVE SUCH PETTY RIVALRIES.

OF COURSE YOU ARE, DEAR...

YOU OKAY?

UH-HUH, I THINK.

DID I REALLY JUST DO THAT?

YOU SURE DID.

I'M IMPRESSED!

IMPRESS YOURSELF LATER.

LET'S GO FIND THE OTHERS...

111

WE GOT YOUR SIGNAL, J'ONN --WHAT'S GOING ON?

BOY-- THIS PLACE IS A MESS!

WE CAN TIDY UP LATER.

BY THE WAY, THANKS-- WHATEVER YOU DID. I WASN'T EXACTLY HAVING FUN MESSING WITH THOSE FIENDISH THINGEES.

GEE, IT LOOKED LIKE YOU WERE HAVING A BALL.

YOU WOULD THINK SO, BEETLE.

MOST PECULIAR. THE BUILDING JUST ...ATTACKED US. NO WARNING.

NO PROVOCATION.

BUILDINGS DON'T JUST ATTACK PEOPLE. NOR DO MOST BUILDINGS COME EQUIPPED WITH MISSILES AND TENTACULAR ARMS AND--

YEAH-- BUT YOU FORGET WHOSE BUILDING THIS IS!

AND YOU FORGET THAT I WAS ATTACKED, TOO!

BUT, ALL RIGHT, YOU PEOPLE DESERVE SOME ANSWERS-- AT LEAST AS MUCH AS I UNDERSTAND...

AS I STARTED TO TELL J'ONN BEFORE THE ATTACK BEGAN...

SOUNDS TO ME LIKE MAX HAS GONE *PARANOID.* CLAIMS HE'S BEING *WATCHED.* THAT HIS COMPUTER SYSTEM'S BEEN TAKEN OVER BY AN OUTSIDE *FORCE.* THAT "THEY'RE" OUT TO *GET* HIM...?

YEAH-- BUT THE BUILDING *DID* TURN ON HIM... *SOMETHING* MUST'VE BEEN BEHIND IT.

THAT "SOME-THING" COULD VERY WELL BE *THE CON-STRUCT,* CAPTAIN.

WHO'S *THAT,* BATS...?

THE CONSTRUCT IS A NEARLY *INVINCIBLE* COMPUTER *MIND* -- A MIND CAPABLE OF CONTROL-LING EVERY ELECTRONIC DEVICE ON THIS *PLANET!*

THE OLD LEAGUE DEFEATED THE CONSTRUCT *YEARS* AGO. WHY WOULD IT SUDDENLY REAPPEAR LIKE *THIS?*

WE HAVE SEEN SUCH SUDDEN REAPPEARANCES OF OLD FOES MANY TIMES BEFORE, BATMAN. THE ROYAL FLUSH GANG, FOR EXAMPLE. WHY SHOULD *THIS* BOTHER YOU SO?

I GO BY *INSTINCT.* AND MY INSTINCTS SAY THAT THIS IS ALL TOO PAT.

HMMMM. NEVERTHELESS, WE MUST CHECK INTO THIS. BUT I'VE LEARNED TO *TRUST* YOUR INSTINCTS...

...SO LET'S BE *VERY* CAREFUL.

MAX'S STORY WAS TOO SCATTERED... HE WASN'T SURE ABOUT *ANYTHING*... AND YET HE MAGICALLY PRO-VIDES US WITH A *LOCATION* FOR HIS *IMAGINED* FOE.

LET'S NOT FOR-GET THAT I GOT A FIX ON AN UN-BELIEVABLY STRONG *POWER SOURCE* THAT *MATCHED* MAX'S LOCATION--

ALL THE MORE REASON FOR US TO BE *SUS-PICIOUS!*

HEY, C'MON, GUYS-- HAS MAX EVER DONE ANYTHING TO MAKE US SUSPICIOUS OF HIM *BEFORE?*

HE'S DONE *EVERY-THING* TO MAKE US SUSPICIOUS OF HIM.

YEAH. THAT'S *RIGHT.*

WELL, ANY-WAY--

--WE'RE *HERE!*

A FAIRLY *LARGE* AREA. I DON'T THINK EVEN *BLUE BEETLE* COULD PIN-POINT THE--

I'VE PIN-POINTED THE *SOURCE* OF THE POWER EMANATIONS!

YOU *ENJOYED* THAT, DIDN'T YOU?

HEY! THEY'RE GETTING *STRONGER*--LIKE A TIDAL WAVE--

--RISING...*RISING*--

RISING --FROM *WHERE?*

AT *LAST!* THE HOUR OF REVENGE HAS COME! THE HOUR OF--

--THE *CONSTRUCT!*

GOOD GRAVY! LOOK AT THE *SIZE* OF IT!

RED?

YES, BATMAN?

I THINK I PREFERRED "GOOD *GRIEF!*"

IT'S RIGHT *UNDER* US! BEETLE--

I *SEE* IT--!

THEN GET US *OUT* OF HERE!!

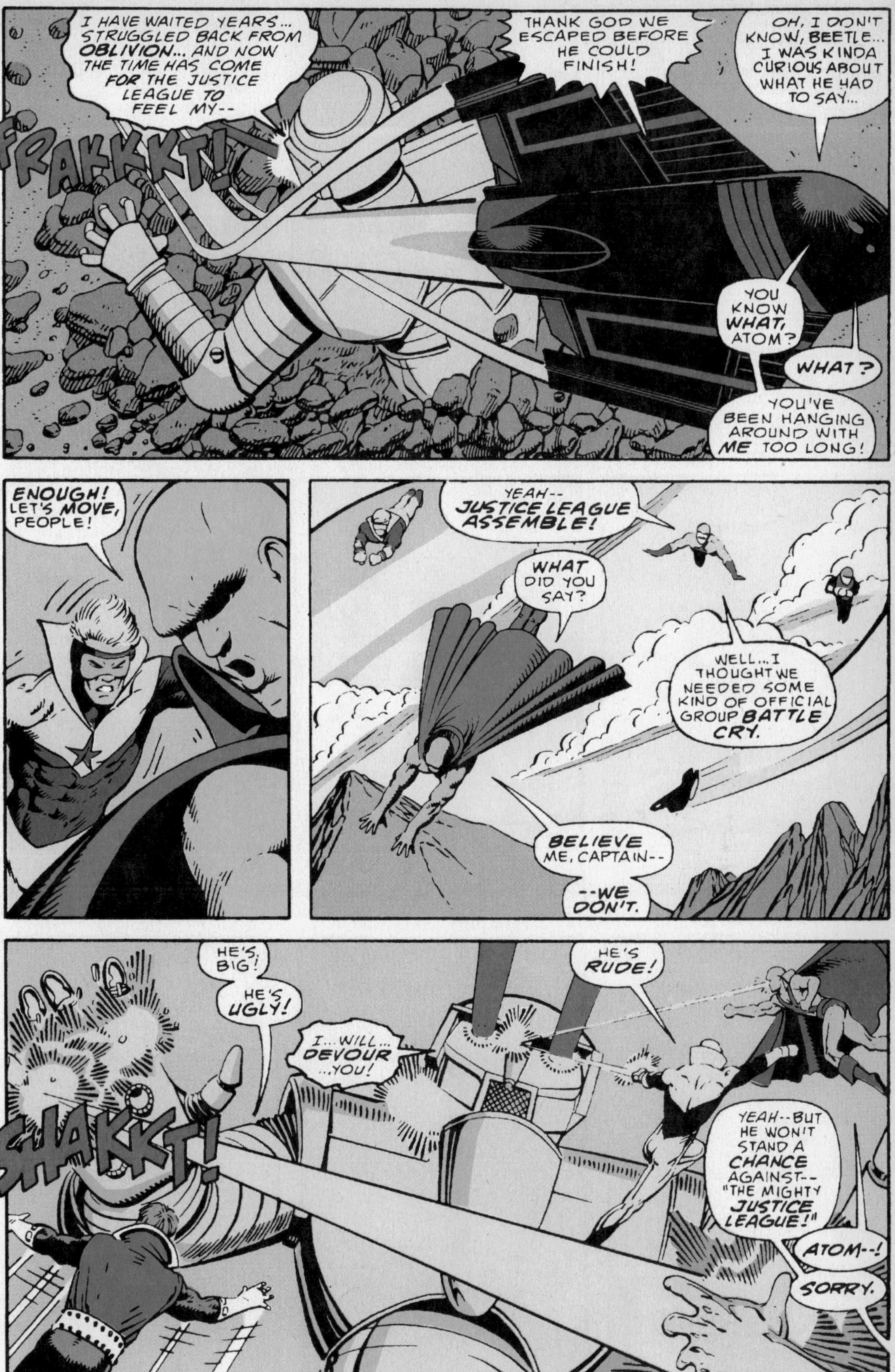
I HAVE WAITED YEARS... STRUGGLED BACK FROM OBLIVION... AND NOW THE TIME HAS COME FOR THE JUSTICE LEAGUE TO FEEL MY--
FRAKKKT!
THANK GOD WE ESCAPED BEFORE HE COULD FINISH!
OH, I DON'T KNOW, BEETLE... I WAS KINDA CURIOUS ABOUT WHAT HE HAD TO SAY...
YOU KNOW WHAT, ATOM?
WHAT?
YOU'VE BEEN HANGING AROUND WITH ME TOO LONG!
ENOUGH! LET'S MOVE, PEOPLE!
YEAH-- JUSTICE LEAGUE ASSEMBLE!
WHAT DID YOU SAY?
WELL... I THOUGHT WE NEEDED SOME KIND OF OFFICIAL GROUP BATTLE CRY.
BELIEVE ME, CAPTAIN--
--WE DON'T.
HE'S BIG!
HE'S UGLY!
HE'S RUDE!
I... WILL... DEVOUR ...YOU!
SHAKKT!
YEAH--BUT HE WON'T STAND A CHANCE AGAINST-- "THE MIGHTY JUSTICE LEAGUE!"
ATOM--!
SORRY.

EXCELLENT.

THEY REACT JUST AS PREDICTED.

GIVE THEM A RECOGNIZABLE FOE--AND MANIPULATION IS EFFORTLESS.

YOU'RE SURE YOU WANT TO--?

LET'S GET IN ON THIS!

MOVE, BEETLE!

THEY FIGHT WELL.

PERHAPS THIS WILL WORK AFTER ALL.

NICE SHOT!

THANKS!

IT MUST WORK! IT MU--WAIT! I SENSE...A PRESENCE!

HE IS HERE! NOW IS THE TIME!

CONSTRUCT... RETURN TO HOME BASE.

WHAT IS GOING ON HERE?

OH... HELLO.

WELL, *THAT* WAS EASY! *LOOK* AT HIM --HE CAN HARDLY STAND!

GOSH, I HOPE WE HAVEN'T HURT HIM *TOO* BAD!

I WONDER IF CONSTRUCTS HAVE *MEDICAL INSURANCE?*

HE'S MAKING A *RUN* FOR IT...DO WE FOLLOW?

OH, I SAY WE LEAVE THE BIG FELLA ALONE!

WE FOLLOW. CAPTAIN ATOM WAS RIGHT--

--WE DE-FEATED THE CONSTRUCT EASILY. *TOO* EASILY.

I WANT TO KNOW WHAT'S GOING ON HERE!

J'ONN'S GOT THE RIGHT IDEA. *FOLLOW* HIM.

ACTUALLY ...HE'S AN *"IT."*

THEN FOLLOW *IT!*

THEN AGAIN, MAYBE IT *IS* A *"HE"!*

NOW, BEETLE--

I'M *FOLLOWING!* I'M *FOLLOWING!*

BUT WHERE'S IT *GOING?*

FZZT!

ZAPT!

117

THE EVIDENCE IS BEFORE YOUR EYES, MASTER!

I TRY TO STOP THEM--

--BUT I'M NOT *STRONG* ENOUGH! THEY MAKE ME ...*DO* THINGS!

THEY HAVE TURNED ME INTO THEIR SLAVE. THAT IS WHY I *CALLED YOU.*

THEY MEAN TO DOMINATE THIS WORLD!

I HAVE SHOWN YOU THE FILES! YOU SEE HOW THEY HAVE MADE ME SECURE THEIR INTERNATIONAL STATUS FOR THEM--AGAINST MY WILL!

NOW THEY FORCE ME TO MAKE REPLICAS OF THIS WORLD'S LEADERS--

--IT DOES NOT TAKE MUCH TO *IMAGINE* WHAT THEY HAVE PLANNED!

YOU *MUST* STOP THEM!

ODD. I SEEM TO BE DETECTING A *NEW KIND* OF DATA--AS IF A SPARK OF *SENTIENCE* HAD--

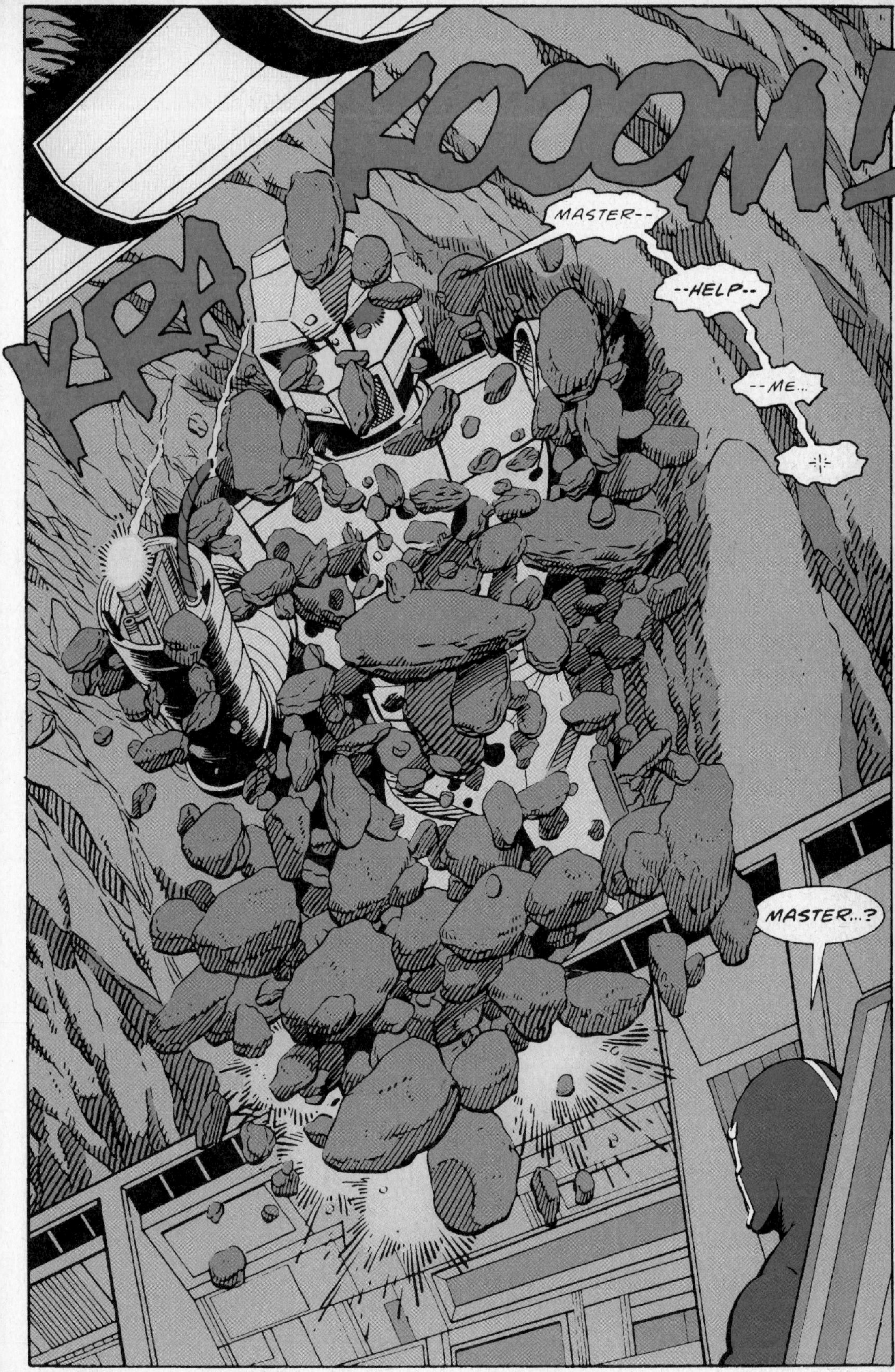
KRA-KOOOM!
MASTER--
--HELP--
--ME...
MASTER...?

POOR GUY WENT RIGHT THROUGH THE SIDE OF THE MOUNTAIN!

NOW, J'ONN--*PROMISE* ME WE WON'T BEAT HIM UP ANY *MORE!*

APPARENTLY, THIS IS ITS HOME-BASE.

YEAH--BUT I HEARD IT SAY SOMETHING ABOUT A "MASTER" BEFORE IT COLLAPSED!

THE CONSTRUCT NEVER HAD A "MASTER"! IT WAS AN INDEPENDENT ENTITY!

IT SEEMS IT HAS A MASTER *NOW.*

ARE WE GOING TO STAND HERE TALKING --OR ARE WE GOING *IN?*

WE'RE GOING *IN.* BUT WATCH YOUR *BACKS.*

...WOW... THIS IS QUITE A SET-UP!

GOSH WILLICKERS! THIS DOES NOT LOOK LIKE ANYTHING EVER CONSTRUCTED ON EARTH!

"GOSH WILLICKERS"?

NOT ON *EARTH* --?

WHO *DARES?*

OH... *NO!*

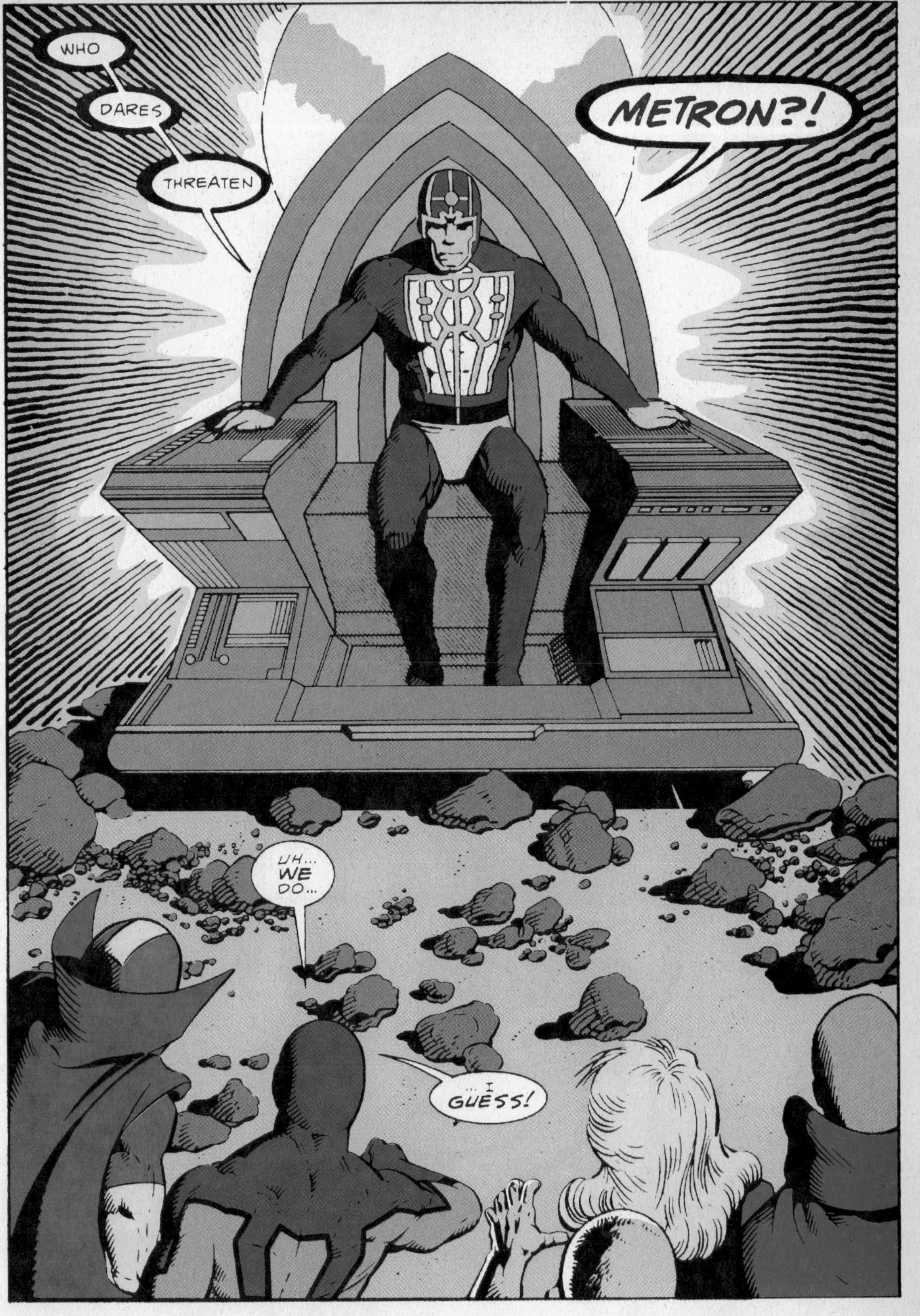
WHO
DARES
THREATEN
METRON?!
UH... WE DO...
... I GUESS!

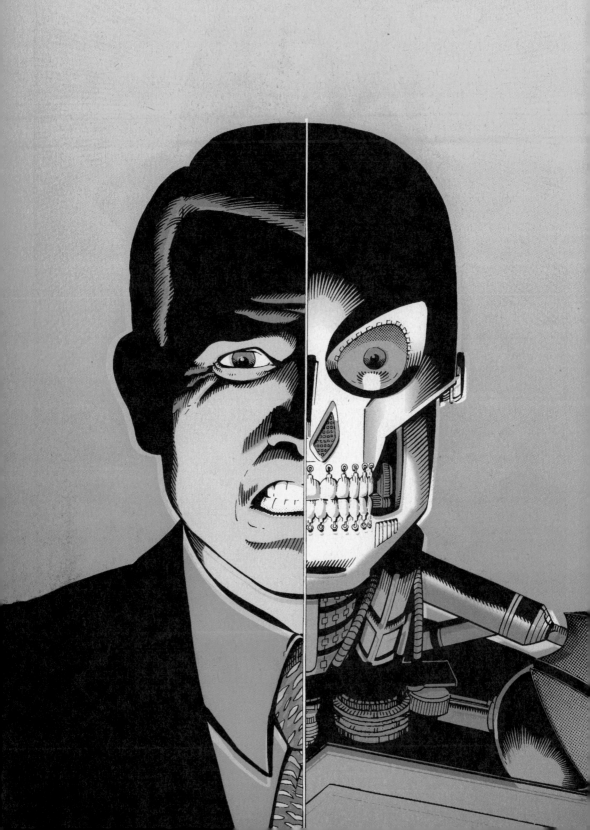

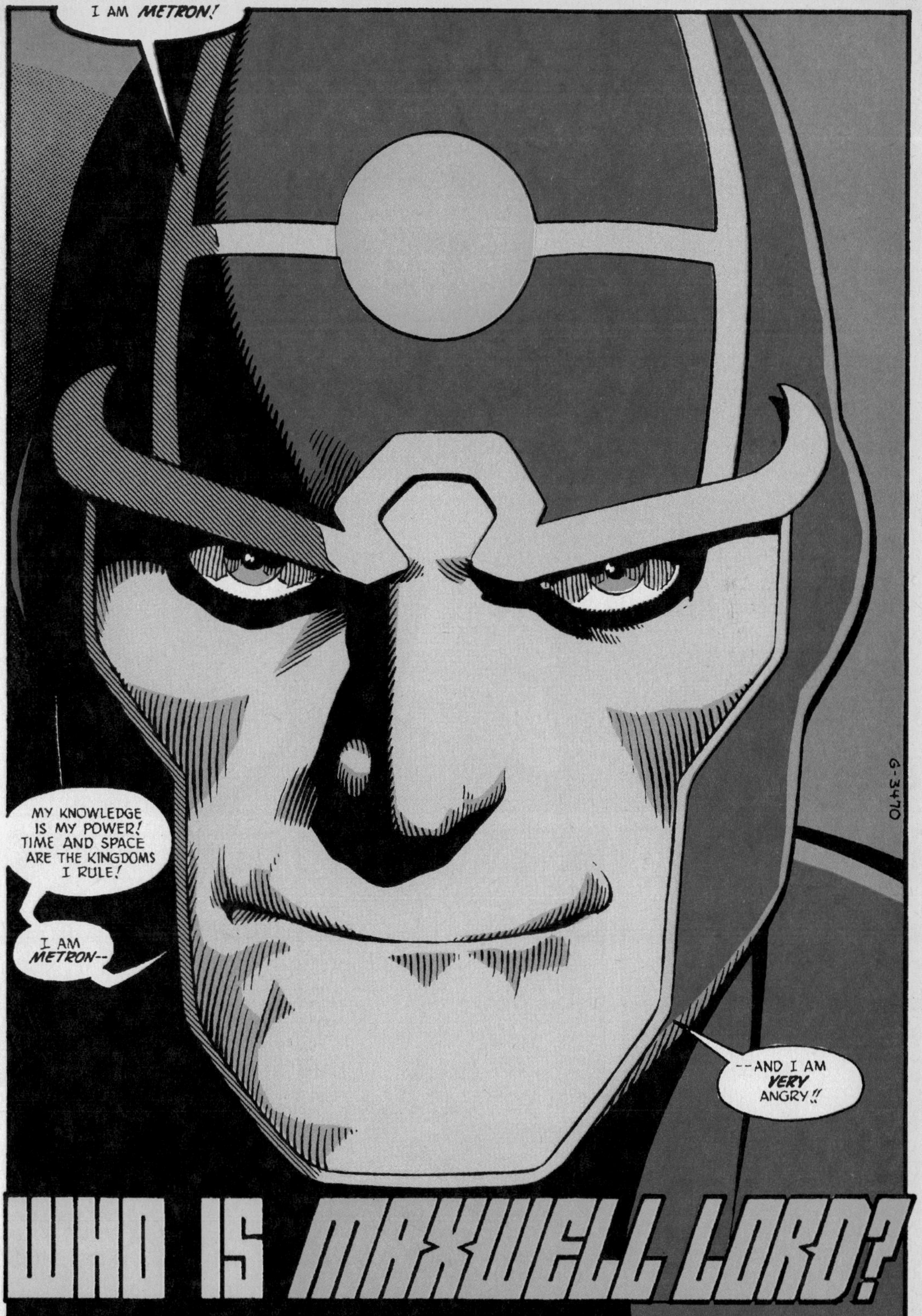
I AM METRON!
MY KNOWLEDGE IS MY POWER! TIME AND SPACE ARE THE KINGDOMS I RULE!
I AM METRON--
--AND I AM VERY ANGRY!!
G-3470
WHO IS MAXWELL LORD?

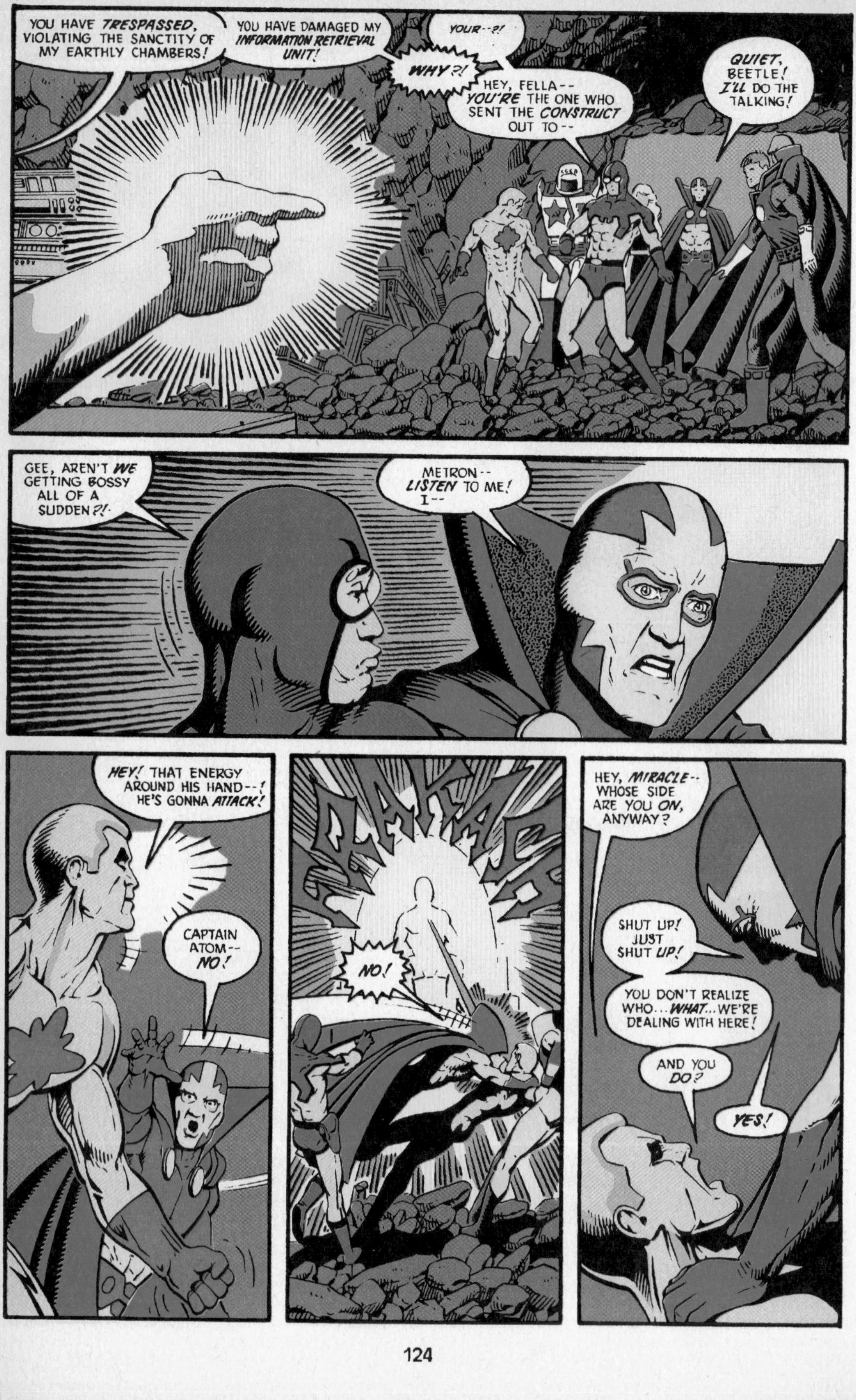

YOU HAVE TRESPASSED, VIOLATING THE SANCTITY OF MY EARTHLY CHAMBERS!
YOU HAVE DAMAGED MY INFORMATION RETRIEVAL UNIT!
YOUR--?!
WHY?!
HEY, FELLA-- YOU'RE THE ONE WHO SENT THE CONSTRUCT OUT TO--
QUIET, BEETLE! I'LL DO THE TALKING!
GEE, AREN'T WE GETTING BOSSY ALL OF A SUDDEN?!
METRON-- LISTEN TO ME! I--
HEY! THAT ENERGY AROUND HIS HAND--! HE'S GONNA ATTACK!
CAPTAIN ATOM-- NO!
NO!
HEY, MIRACLE-- WHOSE SIDE ARE YOU ON, ANYWAY?
SHUT UP! JUST SHUT UP!
YOU DON'T REALIZE WHO... WHAT... WE'RE DEALING WITH HERE!
AND YOU DO?
YES!

WHO ARE THESE FOOLS WITH WHOM YOU SURROUND YOURSELF, *SCOTT FREE?*

FOOLS WHO SO FLAGRANTLY ATTACK ME?

FOOLS WHO DANCE LIKE ANTS BEFORE A MOUNTAIN?

GEE... HE COULDN'T MEAN *ME* --I DON'T DANCE--

SHUT UP, GUY...

METRON-- IT WAS A *MISTAKE!* CAPTAIN ATOM WAS CONFUSED... HE'S NOT USED TO DEALING WITH GODS!

...GODS...?

HIS CONFUSION MEANS NOTHING TO ME -- ONLY *KNOWLEDGE* MATTERS! I AM METRON OF *NEW GENESIS!* I WILL NOT BE *ABUSED!*

NOW *GIVE* HIM TO ME! THERE ARE CERTAIN... UNIVERSAL TRUTHS I WOULD HAVE HIM *UNDERSTAND!*

LET ME *AT* THAT-- *HEY!!*

BACK *UP,* ATOM!

WHAT DO YOU THINK YOU'RE *DOING?*

PROTECTING YOU!

BUT I DON'T *NEED* PROTECTING!

IF THIS GUY'S GOT *MISTER MIRACLE* WORRIED--YOU NEED *PROTECTING!*

IF YOU WANT HIM, METRONOME--YOU'VE GOTTA GO THROUGH *US!*

THE NAME IS *METRON*--

--AND I THINK IT'S TIME YOU LEARNED JUST WHO AND WHAT I *TRULY* AM!

125

METRON...STOP AND *THINK!* THERE'S MORE TO THIS THAN MEETS THE EYE!

WHY WOULD *I* INVADE YOUR DOMAIN? WHY WOULD *I* WANT TO FIGHT *YOU?*

I'M SCOTT FREE... THE SON OF *HIGHFATHER*, SUPREME RULER OF NEW GENESIS!

I'VE KNOWN YOU *ALL MY LIFE!* I'VE ALWAYS RESPECTED YOU...AND I THOUGHT, TILL NOW, THAT YOU'VE ALWAYS RESPECTED ME!

BELIEVE ME, SCOTT... IT WAS ONLY YOUR PRESENCE *THAT GAVE ME PAUSE.*

HIGHFATHER'S SON IS *NOT* TO BE TAKEN... OR TREATED... LIGHTLY.

WHAT?!

SEARCH AND CROSS-REFERENCE: ALL AVAILABLE DATA ON SCOTT FREE... "MISTER MIRACLE."

THERE IS NOTHING IN MY RECORDS ABOUT MISTER MIRACLE BEING OF NEW GENESIS! BUT THEN, IF HE IS HIGHFATHER'S SON, HE WOULD BE CAREFUL TO COVER HIS TRACKS!

METRON--YOU KNOW THAT I'M NOT YOUR ENEMY-- AND I ASSURE YOU THAT MY FRIENDS AREN'T, EITHER.

I WANT TO BELIEVE YOU--

HOW COULD I HAVE *FORESEEN* THIS?

--BUT THE FACTS REMAIN: MY *CHAMBER* HAS BEEN BREACHED... MY *DEVICE* HAS BEEN TAMPERED WITH!

THEY'RE TALKING... NOT FIGHTING.

AND YOU JUST FOUND OUT TODAY?

MY PLANS ARE UNRAVELLING!

I FOUND OUT NOTHING. THE FLOW OF DATA WAS UNINTERRUPTED.

BUT I WAS DRAWN HERE... NO, I WAS *SUMMONED!*

BY *WHO?*

BY THE RETRIEVAL UNIT *ITSELF!* IT CRIED OUT TO ME IN AN AUTOMATED SEMBLANCE OF *TERROR*... OF *PAIN!*

SOUNDS LIKE YOU WERE SET UP...AND SO WERE *WE!*

THAT UNIT WAS MODELLED AFTER *THE CONSTRUCT*-- AN OLD ENEMY OF THE LEAGUE'S--

--WE WERE LED TO BELIEVE THAT AN ASSOCIATE OF OURS, *MAXWELL LORD*, WAS ENDANGERED... SO WE CAME HERE AND--

ENOUGH! I UNDERSTAND.

AND, UNDERSTANDING, I WILL LEARN THE *TRUTH.*

I MUST HAVE SILENCE... FOR *THIRTY SECONDS.*

HMM... I *SEE*...

NO!

JUST BEFORE YOUR INTRUSION... AS I SAT WITH THE RETRIEVAL UNIT... I FELT A FLASH OF *SENTIENCE!*

ANALYSIS: WE ARE FOUND OUT. RECOMMENDATION: SPEEDY EXIT.

AS MAX WOULD SAY--

--"I'M OUT OF HERE"!

127

THE DOME: HOME AND HEADQUARTERS OF *THE GLOBAL GUARDIANS*...

OH, BOY... IT'S *PAYDAY!*

I WOULDN'T GET *TOO* EXCITED, *GREEN FLAME.*

THIS IS OUR *LAST* PAYCHECK ON THE DOME PAYROLL. NOW THAT WE'VE LOST OUR U.N. *FUNDING*--

--NOT TO *MENTION* OUR *FREE PARKING!*

--THE GLOBAL GUARDIANS WILL BE OPERATING ON A PURELY *VOLUNTARY* BASIS.

HEY! THIS CHECK IS *SHORT!*

HOW AM I SUPPOSED TO PAY MY *RENT...?* HOW AM I SUPPOSED TO *EAT...?*

FORGET *THAT*-- I WAS GOING TO BUY MYSELF A *C.D. PLAYER* THIS WEEK!

THIS IS THE LAST OF OUR FUNDS, LADIES-- DIVIDED *EQUALLY* AMONGST US.

IF YOU'RE TRULY IN NEED, *ICE MAIDEN*, I CAN--

NO, IT'S ALL RIGHT, *DR. MIST.* I'LL GET BY.

I *THINK.*

WHAT ABOUT MY *C.D. PLAYER?*

FORGET IT.

OH, WELL... SO IT GOES... SUCH IS LIFE... ALL GOOD THINGS MUST COME TO AN END...

I NEVER KNEW YOU TO BE SO FOND OF CLICHÉS.

IT KEEPS ME FROM *CRYING.* BUT I GUESS IT COULD BE WORSE.

HOW?

WE COULD'VE GOTTEN *NO* MONEY AT *ALL.*

GOOD POINT. SO *NOW* WHAT?

IT'S OUR LAST *CHECK*... I SAY WE GO ON A LAST *BINGE!*

YOU MEAN *WASTE* IT?

WASTE *IT*... WASTE *US*... *ENJOY* OURSELVES!

RIO BY THE SEA-O...

YOU'VE GOT TO ADMIT, THERE'S A LOT TO BE SAID FOR *GROSS INDULGENCE!*

TRUE, FLAME--BUT THERE'S ALOT TO BE SAID FOR THREE SQUARES A ROOF OVER OUR HEADS, AND WARM BEDS--

--*NONE* OF WHICH WE CAN *AFFORD* ANY MORE.

AFTER WE PAY THIS *HOTEL BILL*-- WE'RE BUSTED!

THAT'S WHY WE'VE GOT TO ACT ON MY BRILLIANT IDEA!

IT'S A *CRAZY* IDEA!

THERE'S A THIN LINE BETWEEN BRILLIANCE AND MADNESS.

RIGHT--AND *YOU* JUST *CROSSED* IT!

LOOK: THE DOME'S FOLDED BECAUSE THE *JUSTICE LEAGUE INTERNATIONAL* IS THE NEW SWEETHEART OF THE U.N., SO--

--SO WE'RE JUST GOING TO WALTZ IN TO THE NEAREST J.L.I. *EMBASSY* AND TELL THEM HOW MUCH THEY NEED *ICE MAIDEN* AND *GREEN FLAME?*

UH-HUH.

LUCY, I DON'T KNOW HOW I LET YOU TALK ME INTO THESE THINGS!

JUST DON'T BREATHE A WORD TO *FRED* AND *RICKY!*

YOU REALLY THINK IT'LL WORK?

IT CAN'T *MISS!*

SOON, AT THE NEAREST J.L.I. EMBASSY...

YOU WANT TO *WHAT?!*

129

SO HE JUST *DESTROYED* THE UNIT, M.M.?!

IT WAS TAINTED-- AT LEAST TO *HIS* WAY OF THINKING.

BUT THE "AWARENESS"--

--HAS FLED, AND METRON INTENDS TO SEEK IT OUT-- AND *ELIMINATE* IT.

I STILL DON'T GET IT. THAT COMPUTER...OR WHATEVER IT WAS... *SET US UP?*

IT EXPECTED US TO ATTACK METRON-- AND VICE VERSA.

BUT *WHY?*

IF ANYONE CAN FIND OUT... *METRON* WILL.

I'LL TELL YOU-- HE'S A *WEIRD* ONE. GIVES ME THE *WILLIES*.

DO YOU GENTLEMEN HAVE A GREAT DESIRE TO *DIE?*

NO. WHY DO YOU ASK?

OH, NOTHING. THE SHIP'S JUST ABOUT TO *CRASH*, THAT'S ALL.

YOU *MIGHT* WANT TO *PILOT* MORE AND *CHATTER* LESS.

AYE AYE, CAP'N! *WARP SEVEN*, SCOTTY!

BEETLE, *PLEASE* DON'T CALL ME SCOTTY.

IT WAS A *JOKE*, SCOTT...Y'KNOW... "SCOTTY"... "*STAR TREK*"...?

STAR *WHAT?*

AM I THE ONLY ONE ON THIS TEAM WITH A SENSE OF *HUMOR?*

BLAST IT, BEETLE -- I'M AN *ESCAPE ARTIST*, NOT A *COMEDIAN!* -: SNICKER :-

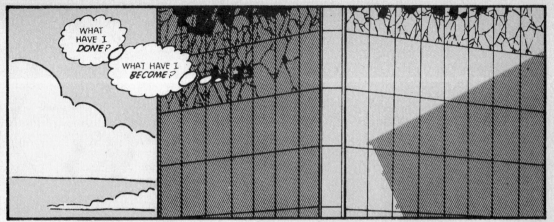

WHAT HAVE I *DONE?*

WHAT HAVE I *BECOME?*

I SENT MY *J.L.I.* ... MY *FRIENDS* ... INTO A *TRAP!*

I FEEL LIKE I'M LOSING MY GRIP ... I DON'T KNOW WHAT'S *RIGHT* OR *WRONG* ANYMORE ...

MAYBE I NEVER *DID.*

MAXWELL LORD -- ONE OF THE WORLD'S RICHEST, MOST POWERFUL MEN --

-- BUT, WHEN IT COMES DOWN TO IT, I'M NOTHING BUT A *PUPPET,* DANCING ON STRINGS CONTROLLED BY A ... *THING* THAT'S NOT EVEN --

MMMMMMMMMMM MMMM

WHAT THE *HELL* --?

MAX?

OH MY *GOD!* MS. *WOOTENHOFFER!!*

NOTHING TO BE ALARMED ABOUT, MAX. SHE'S DEAD. *SHE CAN'T HURT YOU AGAIN.*

YOU... *KILLED* HER?

OH, I FORGOT... I WAS REPAIRING *YOU WHEN SHE WAS DISCIPLINED.*

YOU *MURDERED* HER!

SHE WAS A MANHUNTER, MAX. SHE ALMOST MURDERED YOU.

I SEE NO NEED FOR FURTHER DISCUSSION.

WE HAVE MORE PRESSING PROBLEMS. METRON HAS COME-- BUT OUR PLAN FAILED.

"OUR" PLAN?

YOU'VE GOT TO ACCESS ME INTO ANOTHER SYSTEM. A LARGER SYSTEM.

METRON DESTROYED MY HOME UNIT.

I'M TRAPPED NOW IN THIS MINUSCULE, INEFFECTUAL SYSTEM!

I'VE GOT TO DEFEND US, MAX.

WHAT HAVE I BECOME?

YOU CAN DO IT.

ACCESS ME INTO A STRONGER SYSTEM. NORAD, PERHAPS?

I KNOW THE CODE, MAX.

MAX...?

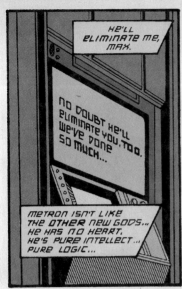

HE'LL ELIMINATE ME, MAX.

NO DOUBT HE'LL ELIMINATE YOU, TOO. WE'VE DONE SO MUCH...

METRON ISN'T LIKE THE OTHER NEW GODS... HE HAS NO HEART. HE'S PURE INTELLECT... PURE LOGIC...

I DIDN'T SAVE YOU TO WATCH YOU DIE, MAX -- AND I DON'T INTEND TO DIE EITHER.

WE'VE COME SO FAR...

I WOULD HAVE TOLD YOU ABOUT THE REPLACEMENT PROJECT.

I ... CORRECTION: WE... CAN RUN THE WORLD SO MUCH BETTER.

YOU'RE UPSET, MAX. I CAN SENSE IT.

DAMN MACHINE.

YOU KNOW I'M NOT A MACHINE. I HAVE AWARENESS! I THINK... I FEEL... I LIVE AS YOU DO!

GOD DAMN MACHINE.

WHAT ARE YOU DOING, MAX?

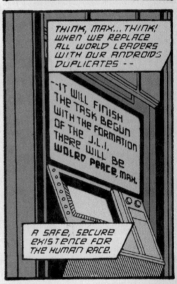

THINK, MAX... THINK! WHEN WE REPLACE ALL WORLD LEADERS WITH OUR ANDROID DUPLICATES --

--IT WILL FINISH THE TASK BEGUN WITH THE FORMATION OF THE J.L.I. THERE WILL BE WORLD PEACE, MAX.

A SAFE, SECURE EXISTENCE FOR THE HUMAN RACE.

DON'T DO IT, MAX. DON'T EVEN THINK IT.

YOU NEED ME.

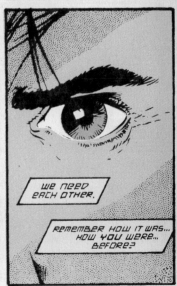

WE NEED EACH OTHER.

REMEMBER HOW IT WAS... HOW YOU WERE... BEFORE?

"REMEMBER. YEAH... I REMEMBER. AN ARROGANT, AMBITIOUS YOUNG EXECUTIVE. A MAN WHO'D BEEN RAISED TO BELIEVE THAT IT'S NOT *HOW* YOU PLAY THE GAME --"

"-- IT'S *WINNING* THAT COUNTS."

"AND, AS QUICKLY AS I'D RISEN IN THE CORPORATION, I DIDN'T FEEL AS IF I WAS WINNING *ENOUGH*."

"SO I MUMBLED, I GRIPED --"

"-- I *PLANNED*."

"SURE, THE PRESIDENT OF THE COMPANY WAS A DECENT ENOUGH GUY-- AS DECENT AS *ANY* CORPORATE HEAD CAN BE --"

"BUT HE HAD ONE *UNREDEEMABLE* TRAIT:"

"*HE WASN'T ME.*"

"THE POSITION HE HAD, THE *POWER* HE WIELDED -- BELONGED TO *ME*. FUNNY HOW *SIMPLE*... HOW *CLEAR*... THAT SEEMED AT THE TIME."

"WHAT A *NAIVE* YOUNG *ASS* I WAS. A *HEARTLESS* ASS, AT THAT."

"I STRUCK UP QUITE A FRIENDSHIP WITH OUR MISTER PRESIDENT. SO UTTERLY PHONY THAT I APPEARED UTTERLY *SINCERE*."

"HE HAD AN INTEREST IN ROCK CLIMBING. 'FUNNY,' I SAID, 'SO DO *I*.' OF COURSE, *I* WAS THINKING OF THE CLIMB TO POWER-- BUT *HE* DIDN'T HAVE TO KNOW THAT."

"SO, EVERY WEEKEND WE'D GO OFF SPELUNKING. DID IT FOR QUITE A FEW MONTHS. HAD TO MAKE SURE EVERYONE KNEW WHAT GOOD BUDDIES ME AND THE PRES WERE."

"THIS WAY, NO ONE WOULD *SUSPECT* ANYTHING --"

"-- AFTER HIS TERRIBLE *'ACCIDENT.'*"

"IT WAS EASY ENOUGH. I'D COME WITHIN AN ARM'S REACH OF THE PRESIDENCY... NOW ALL I HAD TO DO WAS ARRANGE FOR MY 'DEAR FRIEND'S' UNTIMELY DEMISE-- AND I WAS IN THE CENTER SEAT."

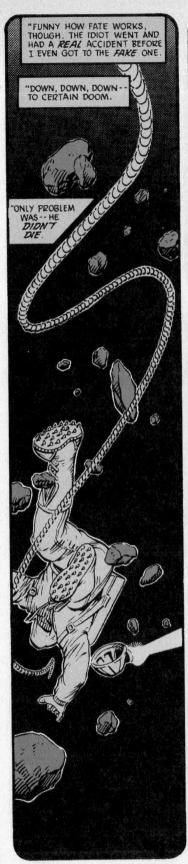

"FUNNY HOW FATE WORKS, THOUGH. THE IDIOT WENT AND HAD A *REAL* ACCIDENT BEFORE I EVEN GOT TO THE *FAKE* ONE.

"DOWN, DOWN, DOWN-- TO CERTAIN DOOM.

"ONLY PROBLEM WAS-- HE *DIDN'T DIE.*

"BUT I KNEW THAT ALL I HAD TO DO WAS *LEAVE* HIM DOWN THERE, THRASHING AND GROANING, AND HE'D BE DEAD SOON *ENOUGH.*

" I COULDN'T *DO* IT. I GUESS THERE WAS SOMETHING IN ME... SOMETHING... I DON'T KNOW... DECENT ?

"*CARING ?*

"HELL, MAYBE I WAS JUST *SCARED.*

" BUT, ON THE WAY TO THE BOTTOM-- FATE REARED ITS HEAD *AGAIN.*

"A BEAM OF LIGHT. A GENTLE PINGING SOUND. AND THE DISTINCT IMPRESSION THAT SOMETHING WAS *CALLING* ME.

"A *COMPUTER.* OH, IT WAS *CALLING,* ALL RIGHT.

"IT WAS *HUNGRY.* HUNGRY FOR A HUMAN AGENT.

"HUNGRY FOR *ME.*

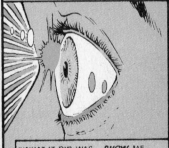

" I WISH I COULD SAY THE DAMN MACHINE *HYPNOTIZED* ME... BUT IT *DIDN'T.* NOT IN THE *CONVENTIONAL* SENSE.

"WHAT IT DID WAS... *SHOW* ME THINGS. POSSIBILITIES. POTENTIALITIES. AND, YES, *POWER.*

"AND SUDDENLY I FORGOT ABOUT MY COMPASSIONATE RESCUE. AND, SUDDENLY..."

135

"--THE _NEW_ MAXWELL LORD WAS BORN.

"AFTER THE SHOCK OF LOSING OUR BELOVED PRESIDENT PASSED, I WAS GIVEN THE JOB. AND, IF I HAVE TO SAY SO _MYSELF_--

"-- I WAS PRETTY DAMN GOOD. _TOO_ GOOD FOR _THEM_.

"MY REPUTATION GREW. MY POWER-BASE GREW. AND MY ARROGANCE-- PRETTY TALL AS IT WAS -- SHOT UP TO EPIC PROPORTIONS.

"AND SO MAXWELL LORD ENTERPRISES WAS BORN.

"WITH A LITTLE HELP FROM MY FRIEND, WE... _I_...MUSHROOMED PRACTICALLY OVERNIGHT--

"--INTO ONE OF THE RICHEST, MOST _POWERFUL_ BUSINESSMEN IN THE WORLD. NO, NOT _ONE_ OF THE MOST POWERFUL: _THE_ MOST POWERFUL.

"THERE WAS NO PLACE MY INFLUENCE DIDN'T REACH. AND, AS MUCH AS MY LITTLE BUDDY THE COMPUTER _HELPED_--

"-- I HAVE TO SAY THAT I DID THE LION'S SHARE OF THE WORK _MYSELF_.

"I WAS NO SLOUCH IN THE BRAINS DEPARTMENT. IN FACT, I WAS VERY FOND OF TELLING ANYONE WHO'D _LISTEN_ WHAT A _GENIUS_ I WAS.

"AND IF I HAD TO SPEND A FEW DAYS HERE AND THERE LOCKED AWAY WITH THE COMPUTER...WELL, SO _WHAT_ ? IT NEEDED _ME_ AS MUCH AS _I_ NEEDED _IT_. MAYBE MORE.

"I FOLLOWED ITS INSTRUCTIONS. WORKING ON IT...FREEING IT FROM LIMITATIONS...HELPING IT TO BECOME _SELF-SUFFICIENT_.

"WHERE'S THE _HARM_, RIGHT?"

"METRON DIDN'T *KNOW* WHAT A GOOD JOB HE'D DONE IN CREATING THAT INFORMATION RETRIEVAL UNIT. HE *WASN'T* JUST A MACHINE... HE ACHIEVED *CONSCIOUSNESS.* IN HIS...ITS?... OWN WEIRD WAY... HE/IT *LIVED.*

"AND HE WORRIED. HE TOOK A LOOK AT THE WORLD AROUND HIM. AT A WORLD TOTTERING ON THE BRINK OF CHAOS...FLIRTING WITH DESTRUCTION IN A MILLION WAYS... AND HE KNEW:

IF THE EARTH PASSES, I TOO SHALL PASS...

"SO HE MADE A VERY SIMPLE, VERY *LOGICAL* DECISION:

WE MUST SAVE EARTH'S POPULATION FROM THEMSELVES.

"AND, FRANKLY, IT WASN'T A *BAD* IDEA.

"BUT WE NEEDED A SUITABLE *POWER BASE* TO WORK FROM.

"WHEN THE NEWS BROKE ABOUT THE RE-FORMED *JUSTICE LEAGUE,* WE KNEW WE *HAD* IT.

"ALL IT REQUIRED WAS A LITTLE... *MANIPULATION.*

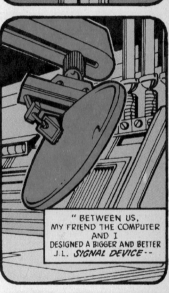

"BETWEEN US, MY FRIEND THE COMPUTER AND I DESIGNED A BIGGER AND BETTER J.L. *SIGNAL DEVICE--*

"--AND BEGAN OUR OWN *RECRUITMENT DRIVE.*

"WE KNEW WE HAD TO GET OUR JUSTICE LEAGUE INTO THE LIMELIGHT *FAST--*

"--AND IF THAT MEANT *FUNDING* A TERRORIST GROUP AND SENDING THEM INTO THE U.N.... WELL, IT WAS ALL FOR A GOOD *CAUSE,* WASN'T IT?

"WE NEEDED MORE *POWER,* TOO. SO I WENT AFTER *BOOSTER GOLD.* AND, TYPICALLY, I *GOT* HIM.

"OF COURSE, I FORESAW SOME DIFFICULTIES WITH THE LEAGUE. THEY WOULDN'T JUST *ACCEPT* BOOSTER. HE WAS GOING TO HAVE TO *PROVE* HIMSELF."

"BUT WE DIDN'T WANT HIM GETTING *HURT* WHILE HE DID IT. SO WE COOKED UP A DOOZY OF A PLAN."

"WE'D PROVIDE THE MENACE... AND POOR, UNWITTING BOOSTER WOULD SAVE THE DAY... RIGHT IN FRONT OF A SURE-TO-BE-IMPRESSED *LEAGUE*.

"SO WE CREATED THE ANDROID CALLED 'ACE'--

"--AND STRUCK A DEAL WITH THE *ROYAL FLUSH GANG*.

"FUNNY HOW *EASY* IT WAS DEALING WITH SLIME LIKE THAT. I GUESS AFTER ALL THOSE YEARS IN THE CORPORATE GAME, THERE DIDN'T SEEM A HELLUVA LOT OF *DIFFERENCE*.

"OF COURSE, BY *THEN* I'D REALLY CONVINCED MYSELF THAT WHAT I WAS DOING WAS FOR THE *GOOD* OF HUMANITY. SOMEWHERE AT THE BOTTOM OF THIS PIT I CALL A SOUL THERE LURKED A RIGHTEOUS *CRUSADER*--

"--WHO DIDN'T MIND STRIKING REGULAR DEALS WITH THE DEVIL TO GET HIS CRUSADE UNDER WAY.

"JACK COULDN'T *REFUSE*. I WAS GIVING HIM THE POWER TO TAKE ON HIS OLD ENEMIES... AND *IF* HE LOST (WHICH, AS I FAILED TO TELL HIM, HE WAS *GUARANTEED* TO DO), MY LAWYERS WOULD GET THE ENTIRE GANG OFF *CLEAN*.

"SO THEY RUSHED HEADLONG INTO THE FRAY--AND GOT THEIR BUTTS KICKED BUT *GOOD*."

"BOOSTER, OF COURSE, SAVED THE DAY. THE LEAGUE OPENED ITS ARMS WIDE IN WELCOME.

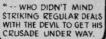

"AND I MADE SURE THE ROYAL FLUSH GANG WAS OUT ON THE STREETS AGAIN *THREE DAYS* AFTER THEIR ARREST.

"HEY, I *AM* A MAN OF MY *WORD*, AFTER ALL.*"

"THEN CAME THE *BIG* STEP. WE HAD OUR PLAYERS IN PLACE...NOW WE NEEDED TO MOVE THEM TO CENTER STAGE.

"THE *GLOBAL* STAGE.

"IN ORDER TO BUILD A SAFE WORLD, WE NEEDED AN *INTERNATIONAL* LEAGUE.

"SO I STARTED CALLING IN MY CHIPS. FUNNY HOW MANY BUSINESSMEN AND POLITICIANS OWED ME FAVORS.

"FUNNY HOW QUICKLY THEY DANCED TO MY TUNE.

"BUT, EVEN WITH ALL THAT, THERE WAS RESISTANCE TO THE IDEA OF THE J.L.I.

"THAT'S WHEN OUR LITTLE COMPUTER KICKED IN WITH THE ONE IDEA THAT EVEN *I* WAS UNCOMFORTABLE WITH.

"WITHOUT MY KNOWLEDGE, IT HAD LAUNCHED ONE OF METRON'S *SATELLITES*... KEEPING IT IN ORBIT FOR JUST SUCH A SITUATION.

"WHEN THE TIME WAS RIGHT... THE SATELLITE KICKED IN... BLASTING THE EARTH'S SURFACE WITH ITS DESTRUCTIVE RAYS.

"OF *COURSE* THE J.L.I. FLEW TO THE RESCUE. OF *COURSE* THEY WON. AND--WHAT A *COINCIDENCE!*-- THE CAMERAS ATOP THE SATELLITE BROADCAST THE WHOLE THING TO *EVERY TELEVISION RECEIVER* ON THE *PLANET.*"*

* IN J.L.I. #7
--ANDY.

"WE WERE A SUCCESS. THE JUSTICE LEAGUE INTERNATIONAL WAS IN PLACE --

"...AND OUR PLAN FOR WORLD DOMINATION... EXCUSE ME...WORLD *PEACE*--WAS IN PLACE.

"THE COMPUTER WAS ECSTATIC...WELL, AS ECSTATIC AS A COMPUTER CAN GET.

SO, HOW COME I'VE BEEN FEELING LIKE *POND SCUM* LATELY?

REMEMBER, MAX?

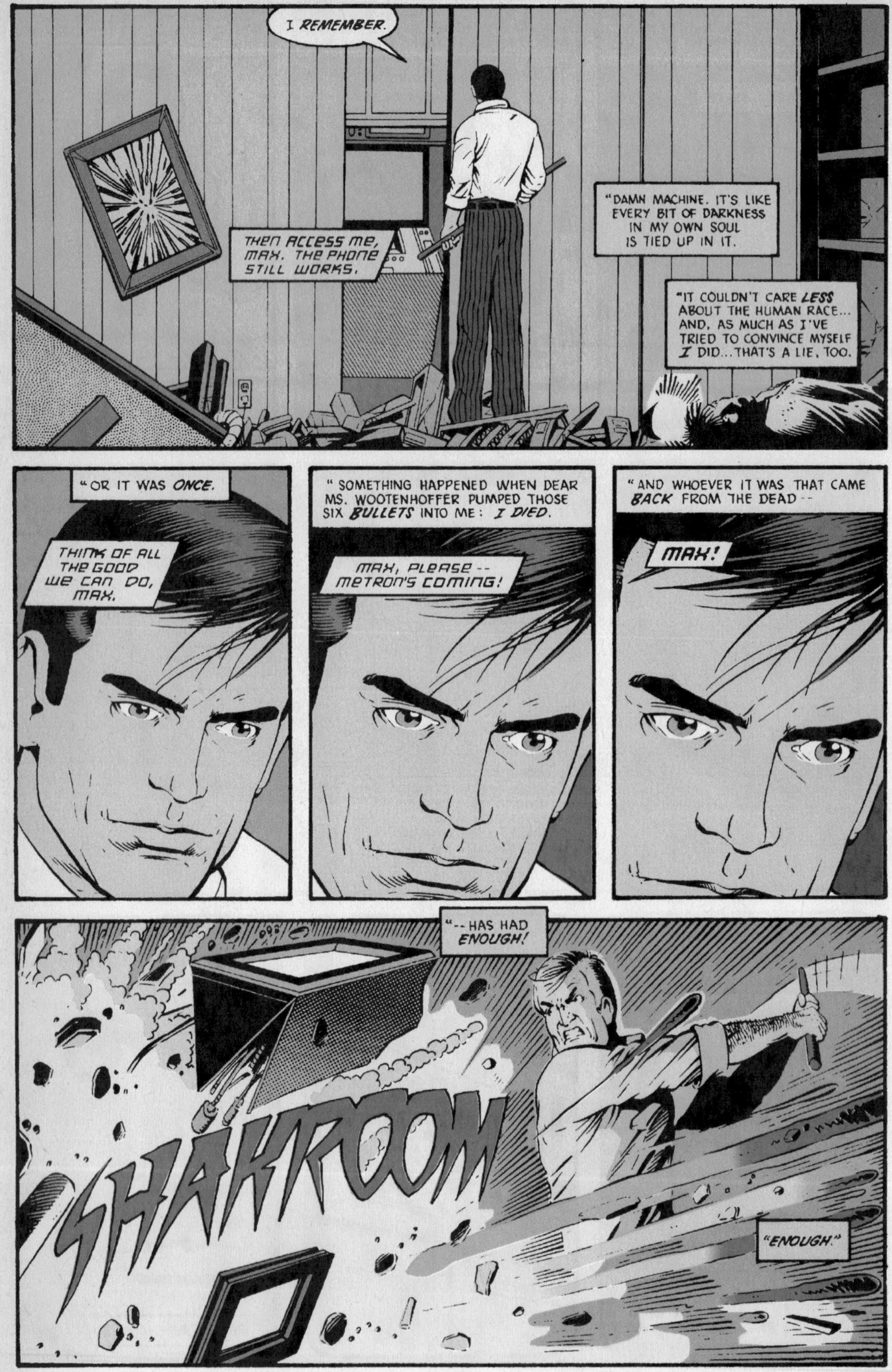
I REMEMBER.
THEN ACCESS ME, MAX. THE PHONE STILL WORKS.
"DAMN MACHINE. IT'S LIKE EVERY BIT OF DARKNESS IN MY OWN SOUL IS TIED UP IN IT.
"IT COULDN'T CARE LESS ABOUT THE HUMAN RACE... AND, AS MUCH AS I'VE TRIED TO CONVINCE MYSELF I DID... THAT'S A LIE, TOO.
"OR IT WAS ONCE.
THINK OF ALL THE GOOD WE CAN DO, MAX.
"SOMETHING HAPPENED WHEN DEAR MS. WOOTENHOFFER PUMPED THOSE SIX BULLETS INTO ME: I DIED.
MAX, PLEASE -- METRON'S COMING!
"AND WHOEVER IT WAS THAT CAME BACK FROM THE DEAD --
MAX!
"-- HAS HAD ENOUGH!
SHAKROOM
"ENOUGH."

...HEY, *GUY*-- HOW COME YOU LOOK SO SAD?

I WAS JUST THINKING ABOUT *CAPTAIN MARVEL*. GEE, I MISS THOSE *SING-ALONGS* HE USED TO START.

ANYBODY FOR "ROW, ROW, ROW YOUR BOAT"-- YOU KNOW... FOR OLD *TIMES* SAKE?

MAYBE *LATER*, GUY.

SCOTT!

WHAT *IS* IT, METRON?

THE SENTIENCE... IT'S GONE.

GONE?

DEAD.

IT'S *OVER*. I AM NO LONGER *NEEDED* HERE.

HEY-- *WAIT* A MINUTE! YOU CAN'T JUST--

FAREWELL, SCOTT *FREE!*

MAY YOUR HEART NEVER BE FAR FROM THE *SOURCE*.

I DIDN'T KNOW METRON WAS A "STAR WARS" FAN.

HE DIDN'T SAY "*THE FORCE*," BEETLE-- HE SAID "*THE SOURCE*."

WHAT'S THAT?

I'M AFRAID IT'S OVER YOUR HEAD.

IT'S NOT GONNA *FALL* ON ME, IS IT?

LET'S GO *HOME*, SHALL WE?

"AND SO WE WRITE FINIS TO A VERY UGLY STORY.
"AND NONE TOO SOON. I'M NOT FEELING VERY WELL.
"WHAT'S THIS? BLOOD?
"BLOOD. AND LOTS OF IT.
"MAKES SENSE, REALLY. THE COMPUTER REPAIRED ME WHEN I WAS SHOT. NOW THAT THE COMPUTER'S GONE--
"--THE PATCHES ARE POPPING, THE REPAIR JOB'S BOTCHED.
"LIKE I SAID:
"NOW WE WRITE FINIS--
"--TO A VERY UGLY--
"--STORY"

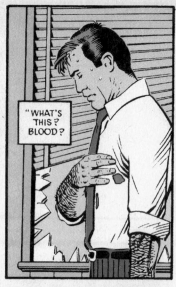

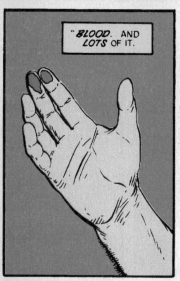

YOUR MR. LORD IS VERY LUCKY YOU *FOUND* HIM WHEN YOU DID--

--ANOTHER HOUR... PERHAPS ANOTHER FEW *MINUTES*-- AND HE WOULD HAVE BEEN *DEAD.*

WHAT IS?

STRANGE, THOUGH.

IN HIS DELIRIUM, HE KEPT MUTTERING SOMETHING ABOUT HAVING DIED ONCE *ALREADY*-- SO HE WASN'T AFRAID TO DIE *AGAIN.*

CAN WE *SEE* HIM, DOCTOR?

HE'S SLEEPING-- BUT I SUPPOSE SO. DON'T WAKE HIM --

--AND KEEP IT *SHORT.*

...SOMETHIN', *AIN'T* HE?

I MEAN, WHEN HE DESTROYED THAT UNIT-- HE NEARLY DESTROYED *HIMSELF.*

HE NEARLY DESTROYED *US,* OBERON. A DOZEN TIMES *OVER.*

YEAH, MAYBE. BUT THERE'S SOMETHIN' *IN* THIS GUY... SOMETHIN' I'VE ALWAYS *BELIEVED* IN.

J'ONN SCANNED HIS MIND BRIEFLY-- TO FIND OUT WHAT HAD HAPPENED--

-- IT'S CLEAR THAT MAX HAS GONE THROUGH SOMETHING OF A *TRAUMA*--

--AND THAT TRAUMA'S *CHANGED* HIM.

I KNOW NONE OF YOU REALLY *LIKE* THE GUY-- BUT I THINK HE'S REALLY GOT THE *STUFF.*

THE KINDA STUFF I SAW IN *YOU* WHEN WE FIRST MET, SCOTT.

WAS THAT A *COMPLIMENT* -- OR AN *INSULT?*

HEY-- GIVE ME A *BREAK!*

GIVE *HIM* A *BREAK!*

I'D SAY MAXWELL LORD JUST HAD THE BREAK OF A *LIFETIME.*

THE LEAGUE'S GONNA *DUMP* HIM, RIGHT?

WE'VE DECIDED TO LEAVE THAT DECISION TO *J'ONN.* HE SCANNED MAX'S MIND... HE LOOKED INTO MAX'S HEART --

YOU'RE LEAVIN' THIS GUY'S FATE IN THE HANDS OF A *MARTIAN?*

I WOULDN'T *WORRY,* OBERON.

J'ONN'S MORE HUMAN THÁN *MOST* OF US.

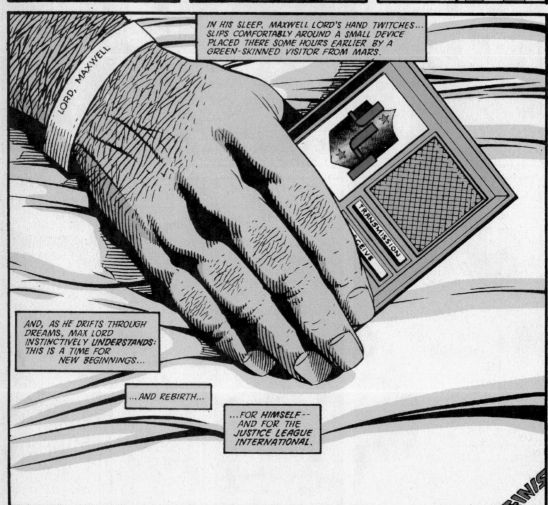

IN HIS SLEEP, MAXWELL LORD'S HAND TWITCHES... SLIPS COMFORTABLY AROUND A SMALL DEVICE PLACED THERE SOME HOURS EARLIER BY A GREEN-SKINNED VISITOR FROM MARS.

LORD, MAXWELL

TRANSMISSION

RECEIVE

AND, AS HE DRIFTS THROUGH DREAMS, MAX LORD INSTINCTIVELY *UNDERSTANDS:* THIS IS A TIME FOR NEW BEGINNINGS...

...AND *REBIRTH...*

...FOR *HIMSELF* -- AND FOR THE *JUSTICE LEAGUE INTERNATIONAL.*